Trans-Siberian Adventures

Trans-Siberian Adventures

*Life On and Off the Rails
from the UK to Asia*

Matthew Woodward

LANNA HALL PUBLISHING

A LANNA HALL BOOK

First published in Great Britain in 2017
by Lanna Hall Publishing

ISBN 978 1 52113 692 8

Cover Design by Olga Tyukova
Edited by Caroline Petherick

www.matthew-woodward.com

The Trans-Siberian is the big train ride.
All the rest are peanuts.

Eric Newby

Contents

Author's note: as most of the place names are translated into English from the Russian Cyrillic alphabet and Chinese characters, the versions vary between sources and over time. The spellings I've used in this book are those that were in the RZD timetable at the time of my journey.

Prologue: In Trouble Again

December 2012

Although the temperature outside is now well below zero, I am lying in the snug and sweaty darkness of a seriously overheated Chinese train compartment. After about half an hour tossing and turning I have a bit of a moment and finally lose my self-control in a high-temperature-induced panic. I feel an urgent and desperate need for fresh air. I need to do something, anything, so I grab my tool kit, get out some pliers and begin to remove the bolts around the frame that obviously keeps the window closed. There are eight bolts, and I remove them one by one and put them each carefully on my table like I'm working on an unexploded bomb. My compartment door is locked, so as long as we don't stop at a station I can continue my work unobserved by Li and Chen, my minders. The bolts are now all out, but the window still won't open. I push, shove and try and slide it in all directions. Nothing happens. Taking a break, and sitting on my berth I scratch my head and wish that I were a qualified engineer. *Why won't the window open?*

I realise that I'm going to have to admit defeat to living in a sauna. But then in a horrible single moment of mechanical deduction, the reason it's not opening finally dawns on me. This window is fixed shut and, unlike the windows in the corridor, has no opening part. What I have actually done is to unbolt the entire window and its frame from the carriage. At this moment there is nothing other than ice and grime holding the window onto the rattling and bumping carriage as we sway down the line towards Irkutsk.

One: The InterCity Kid

November 1977

Like many children in Great Britain I owned a model railway from the age of about eight. It wasn't as glamorous as the ones some of my friends had. There was no *Flying Scotsman* steam engine with detailed Pullman carriages, no futuristic-looking InterCity 125 with working headlights. I was the hugely proud owner of a rather dull green 1960s Class 33 diesel loco-motive and some goods wagons, described in the Hornby catalogue simply as the BR Freight Set. I'm pleased to say that this doesn't seem to have harmed me too much in later life. Back then, in 1977, just a trip to the model shop, its walls piled high with little red and yellow Hornby boxes, was all it took to make me giddy.

A journey on a real InterCity train was pant-wettingly exciting. The big Class 45 diesel trains used to thunder through my suburban station without stopping on their route to mystical and faraway places like Bedford Midland or Kentish Town. I was so obsessed by them that I used to catch a local train to St Albans, where the big trains *did* stop, and then catch one of those to London, speeding back past my home on the way. I felt – as best a ten-year-old boy could – like a real explorer.

There were ups and downs to being a junior long-range rail adventurer. I got kicked out of a pub in St Pancras station after putting Paul McCartney's 'Mull of Kintyre' on the jukebox. I assume was this was because I was under age, rather than the manager disliking Wings. On the brighter side I once met a school inspector on the platform at Mill Hill who thought I was quite special, and wrote to my headmaster to let him know about his prodigy.

I used to meet all sorts of people on station platforms. My railway list of who's who included actors Gordon Jackson and James Bolam. I wasn't a trainspotter, but I did spend most of my pocket money buying tickets to places I had never heard of, purely for the thrill of the ride. To me, trains were a clever combination of acceptable schoolboy hobby and pure escapism. An old man with long silver hair on the television told me, 'This is the age of the train!' and I believed him.

As a student in the late 1980s I took advantage

of the long summer breaks to explore Europe with a magical ticket called an Interrail pass. I joined the community of Interrailers sleeping on station platforms and various night trains trundling around Europe. For a £150 one-month ticket, I could travel north to Scandinavia, south to Morocco and east to Turkey, stopping at plenty of places in between. It was pretty addictive, and I just couldn't put my trusty Thomas Cook European Timetable down.

Sadly before too long, work got in the way and my cheap red nylon rucksack, battered sleeping mat and well-thumbed rail timetable were retired to the attic next to my train set. I felt that I no longer had enough free time to get anywhere that could bring back that long-range rail buzz. Somehow I got over my rail addiction and defaulted to travelling to faraway places by plane for those precious few weeks' annual holiday.

In 2012 I changed career and found myself for the first time with the ideal combination of resources to rekindle my love of rail adventure on an altogether bigger scale – some money in the bank, plenty of time and a large-scale 1956 edition National Geographic map.

This book is about my first ever journey across Siberia. I have included some detail in the planning phase of the trip, as I know it will answer some questions that you, as a would-be Trans-Siberian traveller, might have.

It took me just sixteen amazing days to reach Shanghai. I mention this as many people can get three weeks off work every year, yet somehow the Trans-Siberian is still elusive. I find this a bit strange, as whenever I tell stories about my journey the response I get is that it is something that they have always really wanted to do.

Each year I return home older and wiser from my adventures, but I just can't seem to shake off the thrill of travelling to somewhere very distant and implausible by train.

Two: Midnight Express

July 1987

Istanbul was as far away from England as it was possible to get on an Interrail pass in the 1980s. I think it might still be today. But more than that, it was something of a special prize for the devoted Interrail traveller. To have the journey recorded in your little brown paper Interrail pass was some kind of special badge proclaiming to other travellers that you were more than just a train traveller; you were a rail adventurer. Its reputation was partly achieved by stories spread by less adventurous backpackers – mainly those not straying beyond Nice or possibly Venice. There was of course also the influence of Alan Parker and his seminal 1978 Turkish prison film, *Midnight Express*. But this hadn't put me off, and I remained keen to write the words 'Athens [to]

Istanbul' in my by now quite worn-looking Interrail ticket.

I changed trains in Thessaloniki around lunchtime and waited in line at the ticket office to get a handwritten seat reservation on the daily train to Istanbul. The carriage was crowded, and I shared a compartment with a family who had come much better prepared than me. One of the older children strummed a bouzouki whilst the rest ate a hearty picnic lunch. Their mother took pity on me after a while and cut me a large slice of watermelon. It was considerably more appetising than my stale cheese roll. I must have looked a bit of a state, as I had been sleeping rough on Athens station platform for a couple of days. All I had to wear was my Interrailer's uniform of a crumpled t-shirt (inscribed with something thoughtful like 'Frankie Says Relax' or 'Choose Life'), shorts, fairly smelly espadrilles, and what I mistakenly thought was a rather fetching straw hat.

I tried to put thoughts of Turkish prisons out of my mind as we approached the border later that day. Sat in the sticky darkness of the compartment, I wondered what might lie ahead. I also wondered what my student friends that I had parted from in Marseilles a few days before would make of this. We had been on a university course, and with our fieldwork finished (I think we did more field sunbathing and field drinking rather than actual fieldwork), we dispersed with quite different plans. Some were headed straight home (I assume desperate for home cooking or good beer), some sought European museum culture, and a few of us had bigger ideas. I liked to think I fitted into the latter category, as I was going to travel as far as physically possible on my little brown ticket. I overheard someone say behind my back to an assembled huddle that he thought I was mad to go to Istanbul. The group nodded sagely and agreed that I might not be seen in our tutorial group ever again. I sensed a dividing line emerge between those who sought adventure and those who might be better suited to summer holidays in Bognor Regis.

Back on the train I tried to distract myself from dark thoughts by swatting at the squadrons of mosquitoes buzzing around the compartment sniffing out tasty people to feast on. The grubby walls were covered in the bloody remains of past battles that other passengers had probably lost. Our carriage was uncoupled at the frontier station, and we sat around waiting for a replacement Turkish locomotive. Whilst we waited, the red tape was completed. An official with a rather dangerous-looking moustache emerged from his office at the end of the platform carrying bundles of our passports. Whilst most travellers rummaged through the piles one by one, the British formed a group, and one person, acting head boy, called out names like we were in some kind of school assembly. When he called my name and looked at my passport, I could tell he wasn't sure if it was actually me. Most immigration officials failed to recognise me from the black and white photograph in my big blue passport. It had been taken at a time that I had a particularly strange haircut that could be charitably described as 'new romantic'.

Soon I was back in the carriage whilst the rabble of other nationalities crowded around the jumble of passports. The new engine then signalled its intentions with much tooting of its horn. It had brought its own carriages, and ours was apparently now surplus to requirements. Following the orders of the guard we gathered rucksacks, food and sleeping gear and headed for our new train. What happened next I had only ever seen in the classic war film *Von Ryan's Express* – we boarded the carriage at one end by jumping up from the train track, just as the driver had decided it was time to depart, manically tooting his horn some more.

My guidebook described Istanbul as the gateway to Asia, and in the bright sun of the next morning it didn't disappoint. I stretched my stiff and tired limbs, and tried to convince myself I had actually had some sleep while squashed into that hot and smelly Turkish train compartment. Outside Haydarpasa station there was a whole new world, one that was nothing like the Europe that I had spent the whole of my life in until then. Hawkers shuffled about selling sweet tea in tiny glasses from carefully balanced trays. Everyone was smoking. Old men sat about with well-worn chessboards and smouldering hookah pipes. People crowded past me with bundles of bread and baskets of fruit as I struggled up the steep hill. The street smelled of charcoal-grilled meat and apple-infused tobacco combined with incense. In the distance I could see old-fashioned ferries plying up and down the Golden Horn and out into the Bosphorus. To my unaccustomed brain it was sensory overload.

I would like to have had some more time to stop and take it all in, but my priority was to wash off a week's worth of grime and rejoin the human race. After looking at a few alternatives, I did a deal with a rather large sweaty man who ran the front desk of a small backpacker hotel just off Sultanahmet Square. He looked like he belonged on the set of an Indiana Jones film, and really should have been wearing a tarboosh just to complete the stereotype. Deal done, I handed him a small pile of Turkish banknotes. He looked at me with a big smile and proclaimed, 'You pay to sleep in room, but you sleep on roof!' He said this in loud excitable way, just like his next line might be 'Indy, they're digging in the wrong place!' I couldn't immediately lock into his definition of what a room on the roof might actually consist of, but I was keen to avoid a confrontation. I followed him up the stairs where he showed me to a large and airy room that had a shared bathroom across the hall. The bathroom floor was covered with something that I guessed to be rat droppings, unless he had a pet hamster or possibly a very small cat. Outside the window there was a fire escape ladder which people paying less than me would be using to climb past on to their home on the roof. Before leaving me alone he presented me with a key to the room, and I was relieved to have passed my first test of male Turkish humour.

Over the next few days a familiar pattern began to emerge. My attempts at resistance to the well-polished local sales techniques were pretty feeble. I was soon the proud owner of my first leather jacket. I thought it was quite cool at the time, but its style was distinctly Turkish and the leather was rather thin. It was probably just as well that I had no room for a carpet, as my rucksack was already too full of festering clothes. The other benefit to this unsavoury load was that most customs officials were just too scared to investigate its inner secrets. Not that I had anything very interesting to hide. Some tinned sardines from Copenhagen, a cheap tape recorder, a plastic bag full of roughly produced emergency cheese rolls and most treasured of all, my trusty Thomas

Cook European Rail Timetable.

The timetable was very much 'the Bible', and much more than something you just consulted to find trains. It had a spiritual quality about it, and you relied on it to get you out of any rail-based situation. That was until I lost it one day, after which things were never the same again. I was on a station platform with a couple of fellow travellers, concentrating on securing our seats on the train that night to Zagreb. Bagging a compartment back then involved either sending one person into each end of the carriage in a pincer movement, or sometimes even bundling one person directly through the window in the middle of the carriage as it came to a halt on the platform.

My role on this occasion was the easy one – to look after the rucksacks whilst the compartment was secured using the pincer manoeuvre, and then to pass the bags through the window. The sacred guide was right next to me on the bench as the raid took place. I had passed the bags in but must have been daydreaming, as the next thing I remember was looking back and seeing the train slowly pulling away from me. I needed to run for it, but that wouldn't have looked very cool, so I kind of casually walked backwards a few steps towards the train before turning and jumping on. I hoped it looked like I did that every day. I made it to the carriage behind the one I needed, but sadly the guide was never seen again. For the rest of that trip I felt naked and disorientated without it, and even unlucky.

I returned to England at the end of the month feeling quite the seasoned traveller. I had been living life on the rails for nearly a month and had covered nearly 20,000 km with my little Interrail ticket. I wish I had kept it, but you got £10 back if you traded it in for market research purposes at the end of your trip. Those long hot student summer holidays of the 1980s were simply perfect to get a real taste for rail adventure. I also learned some crucial life lessons. I learned that Morocco had some of the most impressive con artists in the world. I learned that Amsterdam nightlife was largely overrated, and I learned that in Corfu you could buy a one-litre bottle of Heineken beer for the equivalent of just 18p (and then get a deposit back on the bottle). Perhaps most important of all though, I learned to make the most of a good bathroom whenever I came across one. These were vital foundations for me to build upon when I became a rail adventurer once again nearly 25 years later.

Three: The Big Machine

June 2010

It seems that the done thing in any book about embarking on an interesting adventure is to paint the picture of a prior existence in a job that absorbs most of your waking life. I'm not going to break with tradition on this point. The problem is that when you're in the endless routine of meetings, email and redeye flights you don't even have time to realise that your way of life might have become a little too predictable and unexciting. Snuggled under the comfort blanket of corporate life, I found it hard to imagine things any other way. I used to look at the people who gave up their flexible benefits and final salary pension to travel as a bit mad. Until I decided that this was just what I wanted to do too.

The thought finally came to me in the middle

of a management meeting in the office that I worked in on the rather drab outskirts of Edinburgh. I could hear the woman on her feet speaking, but what she was saying was making no real sense. She spoke in a stream of business clichés that were so overused they had become meaningless to me. Her dialect was pure HR, and her sentences were riddled with words like 'engagement' and 'reaching out'. She obviously thought that by speaking like this it made her presentation more credible, or perhaps even her salary more justifiable.

As she started talking about 'improving team behaviours' I looked down at my pad and crossed off the words on my secret game of management word bingo. Before the HR people took over most meetings, the top-scoring word in my office used to be crikey. The trouble was that the manager who was guaranteed to say crikey at least three times had just retired. This was a shame as it used to be a great motivation for us all to stay awake. No one would be brave enough to shout 'Bingo!' out loud, but you had to work quite hard to stop yourself. Reassuringly simple British management words like 'getting your ducks in a row' or 'putting your skates on' had now been replaced by a repertoire of much creepier phrases. All of a sudden the office was full of middle managers using words like 'granular' and 'transformational'. Given the number of times a week I was asked by marketing to take a deep dive, you might think that I actually used to work in the scuba business.

I nodded from time to time, looking round to see if anyone in the meeting had fallen asleep yet. I made some careful scribbles in my notebook. These were mainly a list of possible future travel destinations, combined with a drawing of a rather exotic-looking train. The HR woman finally sat down after what seemed like a geological age, and the meeting paused for a few minutes to recover and get coffee. Caffeine was the only way to survive a full-day management meeting.

After a predictable canteen lunch (only really any good if you liked baked potatoes or lentil soup) we regrouped in our cramped little room to get back down to the agenda. All the rooms were cramped, as the people in facilities management tried to fit more and more bodies into less and less space, until I presume we broke some international human rights regulation. The only saving grace was that we had a window in this particular meeting room. The view was nothing to get excited about, but fresh air, angry seagulls and a grey sky helped to keep me going. I was lucky that my boss was an ex-tank commander, and the rumour was he insisted on only attending meetings in rooms with windows.

Quite a few of the items on the agenda had codenames. Knowing the names of all the various projects was another part of the culture here. It made middle managers feel important that they knew what they meant. To assist me with my own project naming I had a map of the Singapore MRT system. I used the names of its stations to identify all my top secret activities. I used to keep this in my office, but then they did away with offices. Then I kept it locked in my desk drawer, but then they did away with personal desks too, and we hot desked. We did get a coffee bar, some funky open-plan soft seating and table football by way of recompense. But only the people who worked in IT played table football. No one else was prepared to admit they had any spare time in their working day. The meeting rooms were all given flash names, to somehow prove that what went on inside them was exciting. This was life in The Big Machine.

One of the codenames on the agenda after lunch didn't sound very interesting – whoever named it hadn't spent much time being creative, or more likely they wanted it to sound dull to keep it a secret. It was a 'transformation plan' – a cost-cutting exercise which would almost certainly result in more work for the fewer people remaining. In Blackadderspeak, we were about to move Field Marshal Haig's drinks cabinet six inches closer to Berlin. I studied the new structure chart on the projector screen in front of us. Someone with too much time on their hands had been colouring in the boxes and making it look very pretty. My current job was among many that didn't appear any more. Was this my chance to put my hand up when someone mentioned redundancy? For the first time in my career my heart said Yes. The redundancy packages in these situations were pretty good, and I worried they might not be that generous in the future. Those of us with similar intentions exchanged quiet words at the coffee machine as the process unfolded. Outwardly it was business as usual, but by night we worked on our escape tunnels to another place.

I kept my head down in the office and spent my final days filling in endless what-if plans created by the process people. The process people and the HR people worked well together, as neither knew too much about how to actually run the business – just how to keep making their work look indispensable to others. Together they could keep whole departments tied up in project plans. I learned how not to look too keen to get made redundant (one key skill that I had never been sent on a course for) whilst quietly assembling my escape kit. Before I knew it I was performing the office ceremony of handing back my laptop and my security pass.

The transition to total freedom was an odd one at first. After years of doing everything in a certain way, suddenly there were no people to tell me what I could or couldn't do, no one doing a performance review on me or demanding reams of paperwork. I was actually pretty lucky in that, when I wanted, I was able to work in a friend's agency business. This offered an air of semi-respectability about my employment status, and as I would soon discover was also highly useful in making visa applications.

At first I was a bit scared of the lack of boundaries. I really *could* do whatever I wanted. But the thing that occupied my mind the most was what I would tell people I did for a living at dinner parties. It was funny how social respectability in my world was seemingly based on the value of a job title. Not having a job any more, I decided that I needed an immediate challenge to fill the gap, some travel with a purpose. I would just get going and hope it all made sense later.

Four: The Cunning Plan

May 2012

I had of course heard about the legendary Trans-Siberian Express, but didn't really know anything about it. It fell into the same knowledge category as rafting the Zambezi or climbing the Matterhorn – something I felt unlikely I would attempt, so there was no need to know how it was actually done. Then I started to read books and blogs written by people who had made the journey. Most looked like ordinary people on once in a lifetime journeys. Some were going out to jobs or gap year projects in Asia. A mixture of ages, a few trainspotters, a few hippies and hobos – but most seemed to be regular, ordinary people. There was a difference, though. They all looked fulfilled and happy. The more I read, the more I realised that this might be my next travel challenge.

My first misapprehension was that the Trans-Siberian was a single train. I had imagined a great black Soviet locomotive with a single red star on the front, thundering across Siberia perhaps once a month. In real life there is no such thing as the Trans-Siberian Express. Rather, it is a railway line nearly 10,000 kilometres long that connects Moscow with Vladivostok. Branching off this line are other routes, most significantly the Trans-Mongolian and Trans-Manchurian, headed to Mongolia and China. There were actually dozens of trains on these routes. Some even had exciting names like *Vostok* or *Rossiya*, whilst others were just numbers in timetables.

I mentioned the idea of becoming a rail adventurer to a few of my friends, interested in getting their reaction. No one told me I was mad, but they might have just been being polite. When I told them I was thinking about doing it in the Siberian winter I saw a few raise their eyebrows. I suspect some went home to search online for the medical symptoms of wanderlust.

I don't recall the exact moment that I finally decided to do it, but I do remember when I first told someone about it at a local Edinburgh pub. The very act of saying I'm going to do something works very well for me as a way of committing myself to a goal. It's a sort of personal contract that I have to deliver on. So there was no turning back now, time to get on with making it happen.

The first thing I did was what any self-respecting explorer would do. I purchased an enormous map. I didn't go for a modern one, opting instead for a 1956 National Geographic map of Asia and Adjoining Countries. It put me in the right mood for adventure. Looking at its craggy mountains and its old-fashioned place names made me feel a bit Phileas Fogg. I began to stick coloured pins into it and mark up the main routes and stopping-off points. I also started to acquire guidebooks and timetables detailing the various rail routes across Russia, Mongolia and China. The growing pile of books on my desk was a visible sign of planning progress. As a 21st-century traveller, I also had the luxury of some amazingly detailed websites and online resources. Not only could I find the train timetables; there were even websites that showed the exact train configurations and carriage layouts. The backbone of this information was at a website run by Mark Smith, the Man in Seat 61. This has almost cult status amongst rail travellers, and for good reason. I realised that I was not alone in needing to know intricate details of the Russian railway system. We have never met, but if and when we do I will buy him a beer.

I had never been to Shanghai, and it sounded like an exciting place in a Tintin sort of way. Reading *The Blue Lotus* I imagined myself dealing with the Sons of the Dragon and confronting the sadistic Japanese salaryman Mitsuhirato on a train. Carefully measuring out the distance on my trusty map, Shanghai was 12,490 kilometres away from my home in Edinburgh. I wasn't sure if that sounded just far away, or really far away. It was certainly the longest I would ever have travelled overland.

There were several ways to get to Shanghai, but the one I liked most would involve crossing the Gobi desert on the Trans-Mongolian route. The line went as far as Beijing, which would then allow me to connect onward to Shanghai quite easily. The alternatives would have been the longer Trans-Manchurian route skirting round Mongolia to the north, or the more southerly route through Kazakhstan into north-western China. The more I looked into the logistics of the Trans-Mongolian, the more it appealed. A Chinese train served this route, and it left Moscow each week on a Tuesday evening, arriving in Beijing the following Monday morning.

Getting to Moscow looked straightforward on my map, but a few things had changed since it was made. On the plus side, in 2011 the Iron Curtain and the Berlin Wall no longer existed, and there was a tunnel under the English Channel. But on the minus side there was no single grand train from Paris heading east, and the fragmentation of the Soviet empire actually complicated matters. The most obvious route would be for me to get to London and take the Eurostar to Paris, and then onward to Moscow via Poland. However, from Edinburgh there was another alternative: I could cross by ship from Newcastle to Amsterdam and then take a train onward to Warsaw, where I could connect to a Moscow-bound service. I pondered on this. Both were sort of breaking my rules before I had even set them. Was a ship passage to be allowed in a great rail journey? But Phileas Fogg and Michael Palin had taken the ferry to continental Europe, as the tunnel wasn't an option until 1994.

Beyond Poland lay another small problem. Belarus. In 1991 it had declared independence and if I wanted to head towards Moscow directly I would need another visa. I didn't know much about Belarus, but I read it was the only remaining country in western Europe to have retained the death penalty. But to avoid Belarus would involve a lengthy detour north to Latvia before crossing into the Russian Federation.

In the end I decided that I rather liked the idea of taking a ship across the North Sea – it sounded like what a Victorian explorer would do. There was a night train from Amsterdam all the way to Warsaw, and another night train from Warsaw to Moscow. A cunning plan was beginning to emerge.

I had become unused to roughing it on the train. It had been nearly 30 years since my formative Interrail experiences, and I had forgotten what it was like to sleep on the luggage rack or on the floor in the corridor, getting kicked by the guard each time he walked through at all hours of the night. Instead I had become soft, mollycoddled by the luxury of my short holidays that acted as a respite from work. I still wasn't sure quite how rough a train across Siberia was going to be. I was prepared to accept whatever the standard was going to be, but I was still determined to make it as comfortable as ticketing and budgets would allow. I did decide, though, that I would only travel by everyday scheduled trains. There would be no luxury services with heated floors and private bathrooms.

Conversations with those around me about the journey quickly arrived at questions like: 'Do you get your own cabin?', 'What are the bathrooms like?', and 'Is there a dress code for dinner?' I felt a bit like a rookie NASA astronaut explaining to fascinated civilians how to use the toilet in outer space. It wasn't a cabin, but a compartment. (A cabin is to be found on a ship. Compartments are for trains, and possibly Russian submarines.) There were no baths, and rarely even a shower. The dress code for dinner on a Trans-Siberian train was tracksuit and slippers.

I had a bad experience once sharing a cabin with a truck driver on a ship to Tallinn in the 1990s. He chanted prayers all night and brewed coffee on the floor using a camping stove by torchlight. It put me off sharing and travel by ship for a few years. I should probably thank him for the praying, though, as the ship was called the *Estonia* and it sank the following year in what was to become one of the worst maritime disasters of the twentieth century.

So, did I really want to risk sharing a compartment on the train? Opinion seemed to fall into two distinct camps. One camp suggests that you meet some interesting people and make lifelong friends from communal living. The other side suggests that the lack of privacy, sleep, and shared personal hygiene of others will quickly drive you mad. Unable to put the *Estonia* experience out of my mind, I decided that it was going to come down to money; I would get my own space if I could afford it – and if they would let me book it, decadent Westerner that I was.

In western Europe most sleeper trains have compartments with three berths in, but you can also buy compartments with one or two berths for exclusive use, to get your own guaranteed space. This is called first class, but the carriage is the same as the second class one; it's just that you are not sharing your compartment. In Russia there seemed to be three classes of sleeper. First class (*spalny vagon*) was a two-berth compartment, second class (*kupe*) a four-berth compartment, and third class (*platskartny*) an open-plan carriage of sixty-four passengers. In China, most trains had four-berth (soft class) sleepers and six-berth (hard class). However, on one Trans-Mongolian train that I had in mind there was also a carriage known as a deluxe sleeper. This offered the unique possibility of just two berths and a shared shower. Showers are rare things in the world of Siberian trains, and I was quite attracted to the prospect of having one. Little did I know of the problems that it would cause me.

Learning about all these options and different names for things seemed like fun at first, but often ended in some confusion in emails with my agent. Ticketing was a whole new language that I wasn't conversant in yet. The same train could have different descriptions for its carriage options, depending on which country you were booking it from. It soon became clear that I would be dependent on the people who could decode this language and secure the right tickets. I had thought that once I had chosen my route it wouldn't actually be too hard to buy a ticket – but I was wrong. Other than the red tape, this was to be perhaps the hardest part of the organisation of my adventure. The ticket systems in each country were different, and outside of western Europe few were connected. Electronic tickets were rare, and I imagined that people would need to buy their paper tickets at a station counter on the day they went on sale. I learned that in the busy summer months it was often not possible to get a ticket on the train you wanted, especially if you wanted first class. So this turned out to be one of the upsides of travelling in the winter, when most people would not dream of crossing the coldest place on earth by train.

There seemed to be plenty of companies based in the UK who were happy to book me into some form of organised group tour during the summer, but my plans were a little non-standard. It was time to get on the phone to find someone who could turn the pins in my map into real tickets, visas and reservations.

I started by calling an agent that had a website that looked like it was aimed right at a Trans-Siberian newbie like me. It had lots of pictures of people sipping little glasses of vodka in an old-fashioned carriage and looking like they were enjoying themselves. There were several itineraries and some possible dates nicely presented. I got to speak with a helpful-sounding lady, who I assumed had heard it all before.

'Do you want to share a cabin?' she asked.

I decided not to correct her and tell her it was a compartment on a train – this wasn't a ship – but I was the newbie here. 'Yes – that's right, a first class, two-berth please.'

I sensed an immediate change in her tone. 'We don't do that. You can share a four-berth cabin on any of our dates.'

'Is that first class, then?' Obviously not, but I was interested in what her answer would be.

'No, it's second class, but it's actually identical.'

Of course it is, but with twice the density of human beings. 'Why can't I travel first class in a two-berth?'

'Sorry, we've had problems in the past. We don't know who you are.'

Perhaps naively, I couldn't see the problem myself. So unfortunately that was the end of my first potential agent relationship.

The next agent I called also had an impressive website, and the man I spoke to seemed friendly but not as knowledgeable as I needed him to be. I sensed a lack of factual truth in what he was saying: 'There is no first class on that train, sir,' and perhaps most worrying of all: 'You can't travel directly on the Trans-Mongolian train in December; it's too cold.'

Sensing a lack of practical experience, I decided again that it was time to move on.

After a couple more abortive 'You want to go on the Trans-Siberian train in the winter?' type conversations, I found a chap online who seemed to really know what he was talking about. His name was Igor, and unlike the others he was a Russian working for a British agency. This presented a minor communication barrier with his quite good but slightly Soviet style of email English, and my total lack of any Russian. On the upside, his advice was the best I had heard, and he wasn't trying to steer me into booking a group tour. He also offered to book some of my other train tickets and had colleagues who could help with visas. Finding Igor had been a crucial first step.

It turned out that the Trans-Mongolian train tickets were not bookable until 45 days prior to my planned date of departure. All I could do was to assume this would be okay and get on with sorting out my visas. I was in the hands of Igor and his colleagues in Moscow with the big ticket. I liked to think that they had a calendar on their office wall with a big red circle on the day my chosen train would go on sale. I also imagined that they had a man in a KGB overcoat who would be standing in a long queue, smoking a cigarette, ready to pay with a large bundle of barely used ruble banknotes.

One of my early learnings of long-distance train organisation was not to get too stressed about the things outside my own control. There was no guarantee that a two-berth first class SV compartment would be available on the week that I wanted to travel, but I had to just get on with progressing the rest of the plan. I tried to imagine how many other people would want to attempt this route in the depths of the Siberian winter, and decided to find something else to worry about – like my visa applications.

It looked like my list of visas to collect in my passport would be for Belarus, Russia, Mongolia and China. For entry into Belarus and Mongolia I could apply for (rather simpler) transit visas, as I wasn't stopping anywhere. But for China and the Russian Federation I would need the whole smash. I read the instructions for each form and realised I would need a carefully choreographed diary plan to make this work. Arriving at the border with a visa expiring early or not being valid until the next day would be highly unfortunate, and I started having nightmares about it. Several of the border crossings would take place during the night, so the dates I would need to provide were not at all clear, especially as there was up to five hours difference in time zone on some frontiers. Then Igor introduced me to his visa expert and fixer. Her name was Anastasia. She would check each of my applications before they went off to the embassies in London. She knew all the tricks in the book, as well as a few that weren't. Most importantly for me, she understood the different visa validity date rules. Even my passport photographs needed to be taken in different ways and printed in different shapes for different visas. It was all in the detail.

Sat at my desk in expedition HQ in Edinburgh, I started with my application to enter the Russian Federation. This seemed to be the most important one. Belarus wouldn't issue me a transit visa until I had the Russian one issued and stamped in my passport. The form was long, and at times interpreting it was complicated. I didn't get asked very often where my parents were born. Then I had to clarify if drinking games in the Officer Training Corps counted towards the question 'Have you ever performed a military service?' They did. This was followed by 'Do you have any specialised skills, training or experience related to firearms and explosives or to nuclear matters, biological or chemical substance? If yes, please specify'. I had indeed practised defending a central European country from the onslaught of T-72 tanks whilst hopefully surviving a barrage of chemical weapons. I never thought at the time that I would have to reveal this in a future visa application. I then had to list all the countries I had visited in the last ten years, with the dates of travel. The length of this list surprised even me. 'Did I have any Holy Orders?' No. 'Did I have a mental disorder?' Just borderline travel madness. My boss at work was described as my 'chief' (which I quite liked) and I also needed to provide his fax number. Finally, I needed a piece of paper from an authorised company in Russia showing my invitation and detailing where I would be staying. I assume this was to give the FSS (the replacement for the KGB) time to bug my hotel room and record any conversations I might have in my sleep about official secrets.

As I was in the groove with all the red tape, I pressed on with my Chinese visa application. This turned out in some ways to be harder than the Russian one. Sidestepping a few questions about religious and media affiliations, I moved on to the medical section. There were more questions regarding my sanity and the possibility that I was harbouring infectious diseases. After about an hour I pressed the button at the bottom of the page to submit the form. The problem with this was that they had moved the buttons into a new random order on the final screen, and what it actually did was to reset the whole form. Cursing myself for not paying the buttons enough attention, I had to start all over again. There was also a slight Catch 22 with the Chinese visa process. My fixer said that the embassy liked to see evidence of where you will stay, and crucially how you will enter and leave China, but at this point I had no tickets, as I was travelling by train and they were not yet on sale. Another thing to try not to worry about, as there was little that I could do.

The Mongolian transit application was the most straightforward, and if you judged a country's interest in building tourism from the paperwork alone, you would assume that Mongolia valued its visitors highly. By comparison, the Russian application form felt pre-Cold War, and the Chinese one pre-Cultural Revolution. The Belarus transit visa was unexpectedly easy to complete, as it was really a repeat of the Russian one but with fewer questions.

Once the paperwork was off my desk, my only role in the process was to watch for news as my passport flitted from embassy to embassy every few days – hopefully with a smart new visa inside it each time. I had planned my departure for early in December, and as it was still only mid-September I had a couple of months to ponder over all the detail in the arrangements. This was both good and bad. The good being time to sort everything out, the bad being time to worry about problems that might not even exist.

There is something very exciting about pre-paring one's equipment for an adventure. I think it might be a man thing – many of my hobbies and leisure pursuits have involved an obsessive interest in having just the right gear for the task in hand. My problem is that I am a classic overpacker. The limitation for this journey was not to be a weight allowance (I would not be flying until my return journey), but instead how much I could physically carry.

Small piles of clothing and equipment grew in my study as I pondered over what I needed to wear, what to eat and what to do with all that time on the train. Before long, my study wasn't big enough, so I started to use the stairs. This had the added bonus of allowing me to casually prove to anyone visiting me that I was now an explorer in training. After a while I realised that the pile was too big to find anything in it, so my solution was to break it into three smaller piles. A pile for what I regarded as essential items, a pile for helpful items, and a very large pile for luxuries, toys and gadgets. But before I could go any further with the packing process I needed to find some bags.

With hindsight I was an easy victim of luggage marketing. I must have had a latent desire to look like an Everest-bound mountaineer heading off on a climb up an improbable face of a faraway-sounding peak. I decided that I needed one of those big 'base camp' duffel bags – the type that you could carry on your back, or better still that would be carried by your sherpa. With this in mind I headed to Jenners department store in Edinburgh and the largest luggage department in the city. I must have spent an hour or two opening bags and zipping them back up again whilst looking thoughtful. The staff looked on from a careful distance and I suspect that they had me down as a luggage fetishist. They sent a man over to enquire if he could help me. I suspect he had been selected as the one most qualified in dealing with weird people. He looked a bit relieved when I said I was okay on my own for the time being.

I kept finding bags that looked easy to carry but turned out to be too small inside or too flimsy, or both. I was in search of the bag equivalent of Dr Who's Tardis. I was disappointed to find that luggage boffins had not yet cracked time and relative dimensions in luggage, so I settled for something I felt a mountaineer would choose. I added to this a wheeled carry-on bag, and a third, smaller, bag to carry my rations. Finally for good measure I added a messenger bag that would act as my mobile office. I worked out that I could wear this on my front like an emergency parachute with the big bag on my back, leaving me one arm each for the other two bags. It would have been a good idea at this stage to go for a short walk carrying them all, but I didn't think about this until much later. I was far too focused on volume, and not at all focused on portability.

I had little idea what I was going to need to wear, apart from a down outer jacket, the sort people wear at Everest basecamp. I added to this a range of tracksuits and underlayers, mainly in dark colours, in the hope that they would not look too bad when unwashed for a week or two. An urgent acquisition once in Moscow would be an *ushanka* hat, as worn by the Soviet military in winter. They were made of fur and had earflaps, something I was sure would be prove to be useful, and also looked casually cool in a James Bond villain sort of way. I didn't know then that nearly the whole population of Russia goes for this look.

I had a few old pairs of boots at home and I

tried each of them on, wondering which would be best at keeping my feet warm. After nearly crippling myself on a short walk in an old pair of climbing boots, I ended up choosing a trusty pair of Timberlands. When I looked at them they said 'desert' to me rather than ice and snow, but they seemed to grip better than anything else I had – on slippery pavements, at least, rather than rock faces.

Food sounded important, not just for sustenance but for keeping my morale high. I knew that there was going to be a restaurant car on most of the trains, but had no idea of the practicalities of when it would be open, what it would serve, or how much edible things might cost. I tried to imagine spending a couple of weeks living off what was once a British Rail buffet car, and decided I would also need to plan for some self-catering. I also wasn't sure what would be available in any shops en route, so I packed as much as I dared carry at home. This included porridge, instant noodles, cereal bars and a small range of dead animals preserved in tins. Coffee is a big thing for me, so I found one of those big plastic filters and bought some filter papers and a sealed tin of ground coffee.

Part of the folklore of travelling on a Siberian train is around consuming the odd glass of vodka. I didn't drink vodka, so I decided to import a bottle of Scotch whisky and a cheap box of

Spanish red wine. These slotted nicely into my wheeled bag, which immediately took on the purpose of being my mobile drinks cabinet. I reasoned that every explorer needs a drinks cabinet, even if only to keep malaria and scurvy at bay.

I decided to make an appointment to see my doctor, feeling guilty about taking up much of his time from looking after those who were less well than myself. My five-minute consultation involved him printing out and signing a small pile of prescriptions, whilst occasionally glancing at maps in a vintage travel medication book. The prescriptions were mainly for antibiotics, sleeping pills and painkillers. I had read that codeine was unavailable in Russia (too many addicts), and that in China many antibiotics are counterfeit and might be useless. So I now had a big plastic box that contained a week's supply of most common medications and a few more serious ones. This reminded me that I also needed to get my inoculations up to date, and I booked into the travel clinic for a few boosters. I couldn't get a rabies booster. I'm not sure if this was because it was in short supply, or now deemed unnecessary to travellers like me. Either way I would keep my distance from any barking hounds.

Seeing the pile of equipment and rations grow gave me a tangible feeling that something was happening, despite most of the hard work being done in London and Moscow by my agent. As the weeks ticked by my visas were progressively all sorted, and I started to get confirmations that some of my tickets had actually been issued. International ticketing was a whole new language, and most of it was in German (if I was lucky) or sometimes Russian (more challenging) and occasionally in Chinese (totally impossible). The words were often small, but could sometimes be significant. Shared? Sole use? Top berth? Window seat? First class? Through train? Seat reservation? With meals?

I got quite excited when I heard that my passport and all my tickets were ready. So excited that I decided to take the train down to London to collect them in person. This was partly to ensure they did not get lost in the post (unlikely, but another source of night-time worry) and partly so I could share my progress as a long-range rail adventurer with some of my friends. This was conducted over a long lunch of roast beef at Simpsons in the Strand, and finished off with cocktails at the American Bar in the nearby Savoy. I rather proudly showed them my passport, now full of strange-looking visas. I would have asked what they thought about my quest, but a large amount of reasonable Burgundy had been consumed, so if I had told them I was going to parachute off Mount Everest all they'd have said would have been 'Absolutely, Timmy, you'll be fine'. I should explain that my close friends call me Timmy. It's a long story, but involves *The Wind in The Willows* and an amphibian character with a love of fast cars.

Taking the opportunity to get some practice in as a rail adventurer, that night I boarded the Caledonian Sleeper back to Edinburgh. The Cally Sleeper is a venerable British train, and one of only two sleeper services now left in the UK. Unlike all the other trains heading up the east coast towards Edinburgh from Kings Cross, it departed from Euston at 23:00 and headed up the west main line, splitting on the way so it could serve both Glasgow and Edinburgh. Euston had all the charm of an air raid shelter that evening, but heading down the ramp to the platform I didn't have too long to get depressed about this. Hoping that I didn't look too much the worse for wear, I walked past the ordinary carriages until I found my first class sleeper. A middle-aged lady who did not seem too fussed by the niceties of 21st-century service checked me in. To her I was a passenger, or maybe a punter, but definitely not a customer. I didn't hold this against her; it was more an indication of how long I suspected she had been devoted to serving on British Rail trains. Once my tickets had passed inspection, I was interviewed about my breakfast tray the next morning in a manner reminiscent of *Fawlty Towers*. I opted for bacon roll and tea at 06:00.

The lady indicated that this was a lie-in, and she was doing me a favour serving breakfast at such a late hour. There was no discussion, though, about the wood my breakfast tray was to be made of.

Inside the refurbished 1980s carriage, I squeezed down the narrow corridor and dumped my bag into my tiny but comfortable-looking compartment. It was a very lived-in place, but it all seemed to work. The bed was quite wide for a train, as its purpose is to be a proper bed, not a seat during the daytime. This is a real sleeper carriage.

Next door was the Holy Grail of UK rail travel experiences, and I was going there straight away – the Caledonian Sleeper bar carriage. Although it serves food, it is made up of several comfy leather sofas running lengthways down each side of the coach. Tableside lights gently illuminate the relaxed-looking passengers, and a charming Scottish waiter takes the orders for drinks and snacks. The mood is chatty and convivial. People actually want to talk to each other, drawn together by the shared experience of the night train. There are gents going fishing, politicians, Americans on golfing trips, and old school businessmen – joined this evening by me. I told them that I was a long-range rail adventurer. There were some sage nods and looks of envy, because these people all loved being on the train.

I lay in my berth and tried to take in the

rhythm of the rails. Perhaps I wanted to change my relationship with how I now felt about the train, as if to spiritually connect and be at one with the rails. My meditations didn't last long, though, as the train kept hammering over worn-out points every time I got close to a higher state of consciousness. I had many strange dreams that night. My brain was clearly trying to process all the possible problems of my undertaking; lost luggage, missing luggage, wrong visas, paperwork not in order. By far the worst was being stuck at a station knowing my train is due to leave, but I can't seem to make progress towards the right platform, and my luggage becomes separated from me in some strange Soviet security process.

Next morning as the train came to halt outside Carstairs prison, my bacon roll arrived in my compartment (on a plastic tray) whilst we waited. A smile wasn't included, but there was a carton of orange juice in addition to my microwaved bacon roll and pot of breakfast tea. An hour or so later the Edinburgh portion of the train arrived at Platform 11 of Waverley station. I probably hadn't got that much sleep, but it was a good way to test that my railway mojo was in order. I was beginning to get excited by the prospect of life on the rails.

For the last few days before I was due to set off I felt deeply apprehensive about everything, and worried about the smallest of details. I just wanted to get going, as I knew that once I had started I would be able to switch my focus to living life in the moment of the adventure, rather than dwelling on what might go wrong.

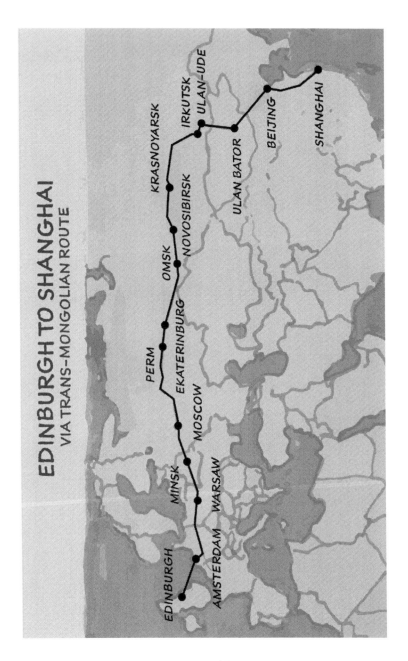

EDINBURGH TO SHANGHAI
VIA TRANS-MONGOLIAN ROUTE

EDINBURGH
AMSTERDAM
WARSAW
MINSK
MOSCOW
PERM
EKATERINBURG
OMSK
NOVOSIBIRSK
KRASNOYARSK
IRKUTSK
ULAN-UDE
ULAN BATOR
BEIJING
SHANGHAI

The Plan

Leg 1
Edinburgh–Newcastle
East Coast/Virgin Intercity 225
1.5 hours, 194 km

Leg 2
Newcastle–Amsterdam
DFDS Ferry: MV *Princess Seaways*
16 hours, 497 km

Leg 3
Amsterdam–Warsaw
PKP (Polish) EuroNight 447: *Jan Kiepura*
17 hours, 999 km

Leg 4
Warsaw–Moscow
RZD (Russian) D10: *Vltava*
24 hours, 1,350 km

Leg 5
Moscow–Beijing
CR (Chinese) Train 004
7 days, 7,862 km

Leg 6
Beijing South–Shanghai Hongqiao
CRH3C (Chinese High-Speed) G15
6 hours, 1,318 km

Leg 7
Shanghai Longyang Road–Pudong Airport
Shanghai Maglev
7 minutes 20 seconds, 30 km

Total trip duration, distance:19 days, 12,490 km

Timetable Train 004

Depart Moscow Tues, arrive Beijing Mon

Station	Arrival	Stop	Departure
Moscow time (GMT+3)			
Day 1:			
Moscow			21:35
Day 2:			
Vladimir	00:30	23	00:53
Nizhni Novgorod	03:40	12	03:52
Kirov	09:44	15	09:59
Balezino	13:27	23	13:50
Perm II	17:30	20	17:50
Yekaterinburg	23:10	23	23:33
Day 3:			
Tumen	03:54	20	04:14
Ishim	07:52	12	08:04
Omsk	11:24	16	11:40
Balabinsk	15:26	23	15:49
Novosibirsk	19:13	19	19:32
Taiga	22:35	02	22:37
Day 4:			
Minsk	00:34	25	00:59
Krasnoyarsk	06:30	20	06:50
Ilanskaya	10:52	20	11:12
Nizhne-Udinsk	15:42	12	15:54

Station	Arrival	Stop (mins)	Departure
Zima	19:17	30	19:47
Irkutsk	23:25	25	23:50
Day 5:			
Slyudyanka	02:23	02	02:25
Ulan-Ude	07:27	37	08:04
Dzida	12:08	02	12:10
Naushki	13:08	155	16:43
Dozorne	16:54	03	16:57
Ulan-Bator time (GMT+8)			
Suhe-Bator	21:30	105	23:15
Day 6:			
Darhan	00:48	17	01:05
Zonhala	03:15	25	03:40
Ulan-Bator	06:30	45	07:15
Choyr	11:33	20	11:53
Sain-Shanda	15:06	37	15:43
Dzamynude	19:10	85	20:35
Beijing time (GMT+8)			
Erlian	21:00	237	00:57
Day 7:			
Zhunhe	03:08	02	03:10
Jning	05:47	09	05:56
Datong	07:59	12	08:11
Zhangjiakou	10:36	10	10:46
Beijing	14:04		

Five: Day of Days

Day One, Edinburgh, Scotland
Distance travelled so far: 0 km

London time (GMT)

Station	Arrival	Departure
Edinburgh		12:30
Newcastle	13:56	

The train was about to leave, but I couldn't see my duffel bag. What had I done with it? A moment ago it had been right next to me on the platform, but it wasn't there any more. I looked around for help, and asked a nearby woman in railway uniform if she had seen it – but I couldn't understand her accent. Ignoring me, she blew her whistle and waved her flag at the driver. He sounded his horn before the deep rumble of the engine and its huge load briefly drowned out any other sound. Then I was alone on the platform, panic rising as I suddenly remembered that I'd already stowed my bag on board the departing train. What was I going to do?

I wake with a jolt and sit up. It was another one of my rail disaster dreams. But it seemed more intense than usual, somehow more visceral. It was like the final episode in a taught drama series on the television. Then I realise why it was different. Today's the day – blast off. '*Don't panic*, Captain Mainwaring!'

Ignoring the pile of bags outside my bedroom door, I head straight to my coffee machine and press several buttons in a well-practised order. Final preparations include rechecking that I have my passport (at least five times), and lots of wandering round the house in a particular order, in case it has flooded or caught fire since the previous inspection 5 minutes earlier. Then I catch myself staring at my bag to guess what might be missing from its hidden contents. Have I developed some kind of new guru power? I give up before actually proving to myself that I can now see through objects, and I call a taxi. I just need to get moving and shed the pre-trip nerves.

My black cab driver keeps his game face on, but I'm sure that he's wondering where the chap in the back, dressed for Everest base camp, might be off to. When I confirm I'm just headed for Edinburgh Waverley station he seems slightly disappointed, but dutifully turns on his meter and off we go. Sat on a tartan rug, I find it very homely in the back, and I imagine that he's proud of his cab. I open the window, as the air freshener is strong enough to mask any late-night accidents. The chilled air helps me to wake up. I take in my last views of Scotland's capital city and its people going about their everyday business. I contemplate how few knew of my plans. One day I'll write a book so they can read about my adventures.

Edinburgh Waverley is a grand station but is undergoing a lot of building work. Leaving the snug and safe comfort of the back of my cab, I move my luggage onto Platform 11, from where I'm due to depart at 12:30. Most of the London-bound trains come from Aberdeen or Glasgow. But today my InterCity 225 is already in the station, as it's one that starts its journey to Kings Cross here in Edinburgh. This gives me a chance to get the obligatory photograph of myself posing in front of the locomotive. I find it mildly embarrassing to act like a tourist in my own city, but it has to be done.

My photo call complete, I look for Coach L (first class), and get the luggage squashed into the tiny space at the end of the compartment. I hope no one else has any baggage, but it's a dog-eat-dog world, and I'm here early. With nothing else to do, I sit back in Seat 47 and read the menu.

The first leg of my trip is just to Newcastle,

with an overnight stop there. It's a small step –
just 150 km out of the 12,500. My thinking is
that it gives me a final dress rehearsal – 24 hours
as a rail adventurer, with the comfort blanket of
still being in the UK if anything goes wrong. It
should take 1 hour 26 minutes to reach our
destination, our top speed limited to 125 mph
(201 kph) by the ageing line south of Dunbar.

When I worked in The Big Machine I used to
travel quite a bit on this particular route. I always
used to take its history for granted, probably
because my journeys would be at the crack of
dawn when all I cared about was getting to my
meeting on time, or the possibility of a reasonably
good bacon sandwich. Today, though, I contemplate the history that places it at the very centre of
rail history. This is the very line that the great
steam trains used to set amazing speed records on.
Engines designed by Sir Nigel Gresley like the
Flying Scotsman and later the *Mallard* thundered
up and down these tracks at over 100 mph in the
1930s. Sir Nigel was born in Edinburgh, and
there is a plaque dedicated to him in Waverley
station. I suspect thousands of commuters walk
past it each day without thinking of the
'powerful, elegant and fast' locomotives that he
designed.

Perhaps my most abiding memory of the east
coast rail route comes from modern cinema. In
1971 Mike Hodges directed a film called *Get*

Carter, and anyone who has seen the film will remember the opening sequence. An ultra-cool Michael Caine travels up to Newcastle on an InterCity train. He sits in an old-fashioned first class smoking compartment dressed in an immaculate Savile Row suit, before taking his silver service lunch in the restaurant car. But the bit that makes the movie so memorable is the soundtrack written and recorded live by Roy Budd. There is real synchronicity with the train as it speeds through middle England before arriving in the darkness of the northeast, where the harpsichord and bongo drums eventually slow to a halt.

Today I share the journey with just a few other passengers and some great views. But there is a strange disconnection between the people in my coach. At one end there is a man in a tweed three-piece suit. On the table in front of him he has a well-thumbed copy of the *Racing Post*, from which he copies notes into a little black book. From time to time he makes a phone call in a hushed voice. I'm not a gambling man, but I bet he is.

Between us are a few businessmen, and then a family with two small children who are equipped with a small army of plastic dinosaurs and other assorted games. The parents seem to have the view that they have reserved the whole carriage as an open playpen, and there are no limitations on the ensuing games. The bigger dinosaurs slowly advance towards my seat. I hope that I will be getting off before being overrun by a large stegosaurus.

The conductor appears at the other end of the carriage and inspects tickets in a friendly and familiar way. I sense that the crew are proud to work on this line, even though their trains are more than 20 years old and the franchise is now in trouble again. I think about telling the conductor that I am a long-range rail adventurer headed for the other side of the world, but decide that this might put some sort of curse on my journey. I keep my more exotic tickets out of sight in my bag. Better to remain the quiet man during these first baby steps of life on the rails.

Taking full advantage of anything that's going free, I opt for the goat's cheese tart from the first class all day at seat menu. The days of proper rail-based chefs with kitchens in the restaurant cars have sadly passed in the United Kingdom, but in Russia and China they are still very much alive, and I am looking forward to this aspect of train-based living. I'm curious as to what the food will be like on the train to Beijing. I can't imagine any self-respecting Russian man wanting to eat a goat's cheese tart for his lunch. Something manlier would need to be on the menu.

Before I have a chance to speculate further on what might make up a Russian working man's lunch, I notice that we were already passing through Morpeth. Giving myself much more time than normal, I pack up, and move my bags one by one out to the vestibule area at the end of the carriage. Missing my first stop would be a schoolboy error so crass that I might never get to live it down. Looking back into the carriage, it's probably just as well I'm getting off here. There is now a triceratops sitting menacingly on Seat 33, and a pack of angry-looking iguanodons have reached Seat 36. As we pull into the curved platform of Newcastle station, the only way that I can open the door is to pull down the window and open it from the outside. I'm a little sad that the country that invented the railway seems at times now to have forgotten about the age of the train.

Getting my gear off the train in Newcastle, it's immediately apparent that I have way too much baggage. I need to climb steps and pass through a ticket barrier, both manoeuvres that I have failed to rehearse. A few people stare at me as I do my impression of a demented human packhorse climbing up a flight of stairs to the footbridge over the tracks. This feels like a workout in the weights section of the gym, and that's something I'm not very familiar with. After a further self-propelled 100 metres I am already questioning the wisdom of the drinks cabinet.

I checked into one of those ubiquitous business budget hotels in the city centre. It was that odd time of the year; not quite Christmas, but when offices pretend it is and hold staff parties before hotels get too expensive. Reception at my hotel today is full of office workers preparing for their annual works bash. Half the group look really excited at the prospect of spending a night dressed as an elf, and the other half are resigned to a party that I suspect they would rather not be attending. I doubt that they will all be looking so lively at breakfast.

The woman at the check-in desk is all business with me until I tell her of my plans. It is the first time I have shared them with a total stranger, and the effect is quite dramatic. Her iciness instantly melts away and after a quick chat she calls over one of her colleagues, as if she might need to provide corroborating evidence to the police if I become a missing explorer. We seem to be getting on well – so well, in fact, that I'm wondering if she might upgrade me.

Then she comes out with it: 'Couldn't you just go on the plane?'

I'm disappointed that she doesn't understand the joys of travel by train. I smile as insanely as I dare, and head off to find my room once she's given me a key to the cheap room I've paid for.

It feels good to finally be on the move, but I'm still apprehensive as to how long it will be until I'm really into the swing of things. The momentum of the short trip to Newcastle has helped get me into the mind-set of living in the present without the worry of what is coming round the corner. I want to become relaxed yet still be prepared for whatever the journey throws my way. When I used to play army games, my commanding officer had a word for this. He called it being cavalier. As he frequently used to explain over a glass of sherry, it was all about being both super relaxed but still highly professional. I decide that I need to think about just a few days ahead at a time. To do this I have broken the journey into legs, and this is useful for keeping some focus and calmness about what I'm up to at any one time. My next objective is not therefore Moscow or Beijing, but Amsterdam.

Having to actually use my assembled kit for the first time, I immediately discover that I have made a few schoolboy packing mistakes. I was right that this UK-based leg is a good final test before I set off across the North Sea. The main problem is making my technology cooperate with itself. I wanted to be able to take pictures from my camera, transfer them to an iPad, edit them in Photoshop and then insert them into a blog, all on the same device. But I haven't tested the blogging part thoroughly enough and I can't upload images properly. Using the exorbitantly expensive hotel wifi I'm able to download a better solution, and get it set up before heading out to dinner.

That evening I pull a few Christmas crackers and drink some decent beer with a couple of friends. I manage to get to sleep early, but office revellers return in the small hours, and carnage ensues in the corridor outside my room. I hate to think what I will discover when I open the door in the morning. I'm pleased to realise that I'm prepared for this scenario, as I have a little bag containing earplugs, an eyeshade and a Swiss Army knife. I decide that committing seppuku would be an over-reaction to the noise, so I leave the knife but use the other items. All I can remember the next morning is a weird dream about throwing up in a Russian train toilet.

Day Two, Newcastle upon Tyne, England
Distance travelled so far: 194 km

London time (GMT)

DFDS MV *Princess Seaways*	Arrival	Departure
North Shields		17.00
Ijmuiden, next day	08.30	

I'm not sure what Phileas Fogg would have made of the Eurotunnel and the idea of a direct train from London to Paris that travels under the sea. I have some sympathy with his Victorian outlook, and had decided at the planning stage that a short passage on a ship would be good for my soul, if not my stomach. I had been checking the shipping forecast for several days before setting out, hoping I would not discover the imminent arrival of a winter storm.

Sat in the restaurant of the hotel, I tucked into my British Isles breakfast like a condemned man enjoying his final meal. It's a buffet, and bits of it are not particularly appetising. Hungover office people are slumped all around me. Many wear dark glasses and delicately sip their coffee, being careful not to miss their mouths. Some need the occasional nudge to stay fully conscious. I suspect that many of them have not made it to bed at all. The ones who are closest to still being alive fetch things to eat for the others, forming a long queue of zombies behind the hotplate. As I feed slices of bread into the toaster for the third time, one of them sneezes into the steaming pan of baked beans next to me. I give the beans a wide berth, and choose instead from a tray of uniformly shaped prefried eggs and some greasy bacon bits. The last thing I need to do right now is catch a cold.

After breakfast I drink tea and consult my phone to see if any storms have come into range overnight. I'm thankful that the weather map still looks free of any scary-looking formations of isobars. Hopefully my passage will be smooth all the way to Ijmuiden, which is an hour or so away by bus from Amsterdam. The sea might be calm, but outside it is still cold and miserable. My ferry is due to sail from a place called North Shields at 17:00, but as a foot passenger I can board the ship any time from 14:30 onwards. North Shields has something of a reputation for being a bit of a dump, so I don't want to get there too early. Instead I spend the morning sat in the reception of the hotel, hidden behind a Christmas tree. At Reception an older man who I assume to be the boss is apologising about the vomit and the fire extinguisher. I wonder if that might explain my nightmare.

I have always viewed repetitive seasonal music to be an act of aural torture. There must be a point when people just go mad. Today I'm a human guinea pig and have to listen to 'I Wish it Could be Christmas Every Day' more than 20 times. Worried what I might do if I hear it just one more time I decide it's time to get the bags out and get moving.

It takes about half an hour to reach the ferry terminal at North Shields on a special bus laid on by DFDS, the ferry operator. As we swing off the main road and down towards the port, my first impression is that the place lives up to its reputation. I would go as far to say that it's a depressing place, but this might have more to do with the miserable weather and the approach of midwinter twilight. The biggest visible feature is a swimming complex called Wet 'n' Wild, which seems out of place amidst the decaying maritime industrial landscape. There would be no reason I could think of to ever visit North Shields were you not taking the ferry, or keen to go for a lively swim.

I manage to manoeuvre my bags off the bus and porter them one by one into the ferry terminal building. Not many people are checking in early, and I quickly reach the check-in desk. The staff are efficient but seem to have little real interest in their customers today. Someone from head office has given them loads of things to try and sell to me. Did I want to purchase a cabin upgrade? Reserve a table for dinner in the Seven Seas restaurant? Book a hotel in Amsterdam? A canal tour perhaps?

No, thank you. I'm beginning to wonder when this might ever end, when she asks me if I wanted to book the bus for my return. Seizing the initiative to break the serve of questions, I tell her firmly that I won't be coming back, and start walking towards immigration control. My plan is thwarted, though, when I realise that she still has my passport. I return to collect it without making eye contact for more than a sheepish second.

The customs man takes a long look at me and decides that it is worth his while to X-ray my bags. One by one they go through the machine and he gets to view a picture of all the weird objects like cans of corned beef and my Christmas decorations. Quite what he thinks of them I'm not sure, as he keeps this to himself. I'm allowed to continue my stagger up the footbridge towards the ship. I'm now learning how to balance my bags without falling over quite as often and embarrassing myself. I wish I looked more like an explorer and less like a mature student on a booze cruise.

The MV *Princess Seaways* is moored on the quayside, joined by a snake-like foot passenger corridor, which passes from check-in and up to Deck 4 of the ship like a giant umbilical cord. I can feel the effort every step of the steep gradient as I climb up to deck level. Once on board I am directed towards a single lift, which seems to be woefully inadequate for all the passengers and their luggage. I wait. Several times the lift opens at my level with the same people crammed inside. They wear embarrassed smiles, out of control as to which deck they are next headed. Eventually I make it to Deck 7, and manage to locate my cabin. It will not be big enough for both my luggage and myself at the same time. Worse still, it's located right next to the entrance to the bar. This isn't good, so I decide to find the man who has the power to fix things in this type of situation.

The purser is busy at the ship's reception desk. He is a tall man with chiselled features sporting a white officer's cap and uniform with shiny buttons. He looks every bit the part. In front of him there is a gaggle of passengers who, like me, have also seen the size of their cabin and had no experience of living in such a small space. As I have worked with Dutch people for quite a while, you would think I'd have got over the comedy value of assured idiomatic English with a Dutch accent. Yet, putting aside my embarrassment that I don't speak any Dutch and that he probably speaks six European languages fluently, I still find myself grinning whenever he says things like 'for sure'. This is good preparation, as the next day when I hear someone at Amsterdam station announce the word 'InterCity' I nearly fall off the platform with schoolboy glee.

A deal is done and I am upgraded to a cabin in Commodore Class. I like the idea of being a commodore, and possibly having a glass of sherry in the wardroom before dinner. Perhaps I could discuss great naval battles and astronavigation with any other commodores on board? My new quarters are to be Cabin 8012, and it turns out this is actually a suite, fitting of my newfound status. The best bit is actually the bed itself, which is the most comfortable I have ever encountered on a ship. The second-best bit is that it also has a complimentary minibar.

Practising my Captain Birds Eye impression in the mirror, I marvel at the size of my bathroom. It's a shame that the cruise isn't a bit longer and also that I don't have a uniform with me to wear. Free of my baggage, I decide to explore the ship. The bars are now slowly filling up with students on their pre-Christmas booze cruise. They mix with Dutch shoppers, who are identifiable by small piles of high street carrier bags from their

Newcastle shopping spree. Outside on deck a moody-looking sun is low over the wasteland that was once a thriving dockyard. The smell here is overwhelmingly of Dutch men smoking what I think they call 'rough shag'. It's not overpowering but aromatic, rather like a good cigar. From my chilly metal bench I can see dockers preparing the ship for our imminent departure. Realising I will run out of phone signal shortly, I swap texts with friends wishing me well. Some also tell me I'm a bit mad. They have saved this news until the last possible moment, and it's too late now – I'm past the point of no return. The ship's lights strung above me blink on, the captain blows his horn a couple of times (in a Titanic sort of way), the lines are released and we set sail for Ijmuiden.

I have second thoughts about dinner. On seeing the eye-watering prices I had planned on holding out for a hearty breakfast in Amsterdam. However, on exploring the ship I find a restaurant called the Explorer's Steakhouse, and it feels like some kind of divine sign that I should eat here. As it's nearly empty owing to the price of a steak, my lack of a reservation is not an issue. Any self-respecting student would be horrified to spend so much on food rather than vodka.

The ship has satellite television, and back in my cabin I watch a few episodes of *QI* before turning in to my comfy bed. Sleep that night is blissful until, just like the night before, the partygoers leave the bar and try to find their cabins by shouting incoherently down the corridors at each other. I have some sympathy with them, though, as every corridor looks alike and I get disorientated finding my cabin while sober. With my old head on I would probably have been angered by the loss of valuable sleep, but now I'm surprised how I am able to mentally coach myself that I need to keep a sense of perspective. I'm sure that I need to build my tolerance and understanding for what lies ahead.

Day Three, Ijmuiden, Holland

Distance travelled so far: 693 km

Amsterdam time (GMT+1)

Station	Arrival	Departure
Amsterdam		19:04
Warsaw, next day	12:30	

A knock on the door at 07:30 local time, and breakfast is served in my cabin. It is a feast of continental cheeses and cold meats, and a decadent start to my first day as a European rail adventurer. Outside I can see ships passing close by, as we are navigating up the North Sea Canal. Reading about Ijmuiden, I discover it was home to the German fast torpedo boats in the Second World War, and the Royal Air Force attacked the heavily fortified pens soon after D-Day with their Tallboy bombs. There is no visible sign of the past today: just a lot of petrochemical plants ashore and a deep-water channel full of cargo vessels.

Leaving the warmth and familiarity of my cabin behind, I give up waiting for the tiny lift and head down the stairs with my baggage to Deck 6. This is done in the manner of a controlled fall, which I try and do without accidentally taking out any other commodores returning to their cabin. Rumour has it that Deck 6 is where they will attach the gangway. I hang around here with the other foot passengers, milling for position close to the doorway. Eventually we are released and pour into the terminal building and down the escalator to the Dutch immigration post. Quickly ushered through the EU passport line, then outside to where a bus is ready to take us on the drive into Amsterdam. I'm sure the bus driver has seen it all before. Looking round at my fellow passengers I feel I am alone in my ambitions for the day ahead. Most of them are still enjoying their takeaway breakfast of vodka and crisps whilst sharing stories of what they got up to in the bar last night. Not having a bottle of vodka or a baseball cap to wear at a fashionable angle, I just stay quiet and hope no one asks me what I got up to in the commodore lounge after my dinner in the Explorer's Steakhouse.

As we pull up outside the Victoria Hotel in the city centre I'm pleased to leave them behind. I wish them well, but I'm on a very different mission today. They have just four hours to enjoy the coffee shops and red light district.

Amsterdam looks a bit bleak today, but not nearly as depressing as North Shields. My experiences so far of this lovely city have been in the summer, but today I won't be sipping a cold beer whilst sat by one of the canals. The coach has dropped me less than 100 metres from the railway station. All I have to do to reach it is to avoid being killed by one of the thousands of bicycles and dozens of trams outside. If you were writing a book about great railway station buildings, Amsterdam's Centraal would definitely get a mention. It was built in 1889 in a Gothic Renaissance style, but today it is covered in scaffold and chipboard as it undergoes a huge redevelopment.

I'm trying to get a sense if this is a safe place. The atmosphere feels okay – all I can see are commuters in a hurry and people eating slightly strange-looking fast food. There seems to be a reasonably heavy police presence, though. I'm used to getting my estimate of how likely I am to get mugged totally wrong. I find New York looks absolutely lethal in places but is normally totally fine. Rio looks so nice, but can quickly turn very nasty. Then I spot the digital sign. It's about drugs. It says: 'EXTREMELY DANGEROUS COCAINE IS SOLD TO TOURISTS'. Not just a warning on the evils of drugs, but the specific risks of poorly cut batches of the stuff aimed at *me*.

Stepping into the routine of life as a long-range rail traveller, I have some housekeeping to perform here. My first priority is to arrange to store my luggage. Then to sort out tickets and check train times, before organising provisions and working out which platform I need to be on. Another of my frequent and reoccurring nightmares (I have a lot of them) is about not getting my luggage back in time to catch my train; I would put my bags into one of those electronic lockers and lose the ticket or forget the code and be doomed to never catch my train. Perhaps understandably I was therefore a little apprehensive at trusting my bags to a machine for the first time. Here in Amsterdam there is a large hall with banks of lockers and credit card terminals. No one seems to be around to help if it all goes horribly wrong. After squeezing everything into a couple of oversize lockers, I shut the doors and get tickets after paying with a credit card. I hope I will see my bags again later on.

With my load lightened to just a single day bag I feel like a bit of a rail ninja. It's too early for my train to Warsaw to be showing on the departures board, so I visit the international ticket office to check on it. What a helpful and civilised place. Everything is okay, and I even learn that it will depart from Platform 5B. This is a concept that I need to get used to: platforms so long that they can have more than one train on them at a time. I decide to do a close target recce of the platform before leaving the station. Emerging from the tunnel underneath the station, I find little to see up there. At least I know where I'm headed to later on, though.

I spend the rest of the day wandering around museums and drinking dark roasted Dutch coffee. I find it pretty hard to relax, though – I'm clock-watching, and I really want to get my first proper rail journey under my belt. Somehow I don't yet feel like I'm a real rail adventurer. Tired from a lot of walking, I find a tiny bar on the outskirts of the red light district and order a small beer. The bar is of the dark wood variety (that's actually a style in the Netherlands) and is occupied by half a dozen locals carefully studying their newspapers. An old lady runs the bar, with her black cat in charge of customer relations. The cat doesn't seem very friendly to first-time visitors like me, so I keep my distance. I sit at a small wonky table, getting a refill of my tiny glass from time to time without talking to the cat. Time passes slowly, but eventually I decide that it's time to put my evening plan into effect.

Ducking back into the station, I find it has become quite busy place now. Thousands of commuters are pushing through turnstiles and dashing for local trains to take them home in time for dinner or perhaps a popular Dutch soap opera on the television. Moving down the outer concourse, I smell something familiar cooking just outside. It's a kebab shop! Given the lack of dining options on the train before the Polish border tomorrow morning I decide to partake of a tactical kebab with extra chilli sauce. Kebabs taste the same to me the world over, but this one contained chilli sauce so strong it would be classed as a chemical weapon, illegal to possess in some countries. With my mouth on fire and some concern for what would be passing through my digestive tract, I fight across the tide of commuters who seem to be headed in every direction but mine. Back in the bowels of the baggage locker room I'm pleased to see that my tickets actually work, and I free my bags from their electronic imprisonment. Relieved that my nightmare was not prophetic, I buy a couple of cans of cold beer from the kiosk and wobble up the steps again to Platform 5B.

I love trains with names. They take you back to an age when travelling by rail was elegant and the only civilised way to travel. My train this evening is called the *Jan Kiepura*, named after a famous Polish singer. But if you were looking at a timetable, you would just find it listed as the Euro Night 447.

I idle some time waiting for the arrival of the EN447 by doing some train spotting. Dutch trains look very different from those back home. Firstly they are double-deckers, and secondly they are mainly painted a somewhat childish bright yellow. With nothing else to do, I watch commuters trying desperately to get onto the packed carriages, and I'm amused to see the efforts that some will go to get onto their train home at all costs. Some manage to make it in the nick of time without being decapitated, whilst others are humiliated as the door shuts just in front of their face. They then have no option but to shamefacedly shrug and accept their fate.

A few of us hang back on Platform 5B awaiting our international service. The woman sat next to me asks me where I'm going. Happy to have someone to chat to, I talk her through my plans. All she is really interested in, of course, is that I'm going to Warsaw, not Shanghai. She looks a bit worried, as it turns out she is going to Copenhagen and we are on the same train. Surely one of us is going to be disappointed by tonight's route?

At just after 19:00 a rather different-looking train slowly rolls into the station and towards our platform. A big red German locomotive with a single dazzling spotlight pulls dozens of different-coloured carriages towards us. I can see perhaps two or three Polish (PKP) carriages as the train rumbles past. Everything shakes, and I'm reminded that this station was originally built on recovered land using wooden piles. Surely it must be slowly sinking with trains like this one passing through?

Wishing the Danish lady good luck, I head off after the PKP carriages, hoping that they might contain my bed for the night. I spot Carriage 181 as the train comes to a halt about 100 metres down the platform. It is painted dull blue with the words 'Wagon Lits' written in an old typeface above the large compartment windows. Old school, a bit shabby-looking, but classy and reminiscent of an age when sleeper trains were the best way to get around Europe in comfort.

EN 447 turns out to be a collection of carriages that will be travelling to all sorts of places across Europe tonight. Carriages will get passed from this train to that, added and subtracted as each one intercepts other night trains. I could see carriages going to Basel, Berlin, Copenhagen, Hamburg, Prague and Warsaw. It was my first experience of a proper European sleeper carriage. When I was an Interrailer I had slept in normal carriages, not carriages with real beds in private compartments. At best you could pull the seats down to form beds, but then commuters would wake you in the early morning insisting the compartment was to be configured back to seats again. The only effective defence was to look really smelly, really dirty and immovably asleep. I excelled at this.

A friendly but busy woman from PKP checks

my paperwork before letting me climb aboard. I guess she has been doing this all her life, but in all that time I doubt she has met a man with as much luggage as me. I wasn't prepared for how narrow the corridor was going to be, and I make a fool of myself pretty quickly, getting stuck as I try to find my compartment. I feel like a tunneller from *The Great Escape*, pushing my luggage ahead of me as I squeeze through the narrow space. All I need to complete the look is a brown paper parcel and a trowel.

My home for the night is a compartment with three berths (42, 44 and 46), but I have booked it for sole use. This arrangement equates to first class. It's small but clean and tidy. I am cocooned in a warm, safe place. I no longer have responsibility for missing the train; all I need to do is get off at the right station tomorrow. Changing out of my winter jacket before overheating, I then wriggle my boots off and sit back. Opening a can of borderline warm lager, I watch people outside dashing up and down the platform still trying to find the right carriage. Looking round my compartment, I decide that this is going to be fine. With two berths folded away, my cabin has a single bed at seat height, complete with a duvet and crisp white sheet. By the window is a small table that folds upwards to reveal a sink. Above this is a mirrored cupboard containing some snacks and bottled water. There are switches for a variety of lighting, air conditioning and a phone charger socket. What more could a rail adventurer need?

As the train leaves the station, there is a knock at the door and the conductor appears. She introduces herself in what I would describe as 'railway English', a language with a few highly specialised words like 'reservation', 'ticket' and hopefully not in my case, 'delay'. Other than collecting my ticket, she shows me how to lock the door from the inside and gives me my own key, explaining in a serious manner to always keep it locked. It feels great to be properly on the move towards Shanghai. No more hanging about; I would be on the move now until I reached Moscow in a couple of days, getting over 3,000 kilometres of railway under my belt. Suburban Holland whizzes past outside, and before long we cross the bridge at Arnhem, heading south for the Rhineland. With every kilometre I feel growing confidence and optimism.

One of my travel pet hates is being stuck in a stiflingly hot room without ventilation. This was a concern even for travel to a place like Siberia. I read that the Russians like their trains to be really hot. But on this train not only can I adjust my own air conditioning, but I also have a small window that can be opened inwards a few centimetres. That's as far as it needs to go. The fresh winter air feels good, but there are drawbacks –

the cacophony of engine and wind noise, and a layer of fine powdered snow that begins to settle on my bed. I will have to ration the fresh air. Preparing for bed, I have the chance to try out some of my kit for the first time before turning in. My noise-cancelling headphones, and the special gas meter cupboard key that allows me to open an unused berth and hijack some extra pillows. I feel a bit smug by being more prepared than a chief boy scout at summer camp.

If you look at the journey by train from Amsterdam to Warsaw on the map there is a relatively straight route heading east. The *Jan Kiepura* had other ideas, though, and we spent the night on a looping tour of cities around Germany. Our timetable includes stops at Düsseldorf, Köln (Cologne), Dortmund, Frankfurt and Berlin before finally heading for the Polish border. Sleep is difficult and I lie in bed wondering how far ahead the driver can actually see at this speed in the middle of the night. The line is banked and the train tilts wildly left and right as it weaves through the Ruhr and Rhine valleys. I dream of being on a rollercoaster. Every so often throughout the night there are short periods of stillness followed by jolts and bangs as the train adds and subtracts carriages.

Everything goes to plan until we get to Berlin in the early hours of the morning. I raise the blind just in time to see the train rising on an elevated track and cruising into the Hauptbahnhof. Outside there are hundreds of coloured lights and a bright opening where the line enters the futuristic building. Inside the brightly lit platform is deserted. With nothing to see I go back to bed and manage to doze off, but wake again an hour or so later, somehow realising in my dreams that something isn't quite right. Noise and movement is a normal and natural part of life on the rails: the sound of the wheels crossing points on the tracks, the whoosh of passing signal gantries, the rumble of the enormous engine. But outside tonight all is quiet. I open the window blind again to discover that rather than approaching the Polish border we are in fact still at the same platform in Berlin. Has the world ended? I lie back in my berth, but further sleep eludes me. I am clock-watching, my stress levels rising as time ticks by. I will have less than an hour to connect with my train to Moscow. What if I miss it? Will there be another train? What about the fixed dates on my visas?

Outside on the platform there is a long announcement in several languages. The news isn't good. If I have understood it correctly, my train is going to be leaving Berlin nearly three hours behind schedule. It's something to do with a delayed train from Basel, which I assume we have to exchange some carriages with. So much for Swiss trains always being on time. After what feels like an eternity there is movement again, and we head out into the darkness of the night. Resigned that that there is nothing that I can do to speed up the train, I fall asleep again.

Day Four, Poznan, Poland
Distance travelled so far: 1,692 km

Warsaw time (GMT+1)

Station	Arrival	Departure
Warsaw		12:35
Moscow, next day	11:53	

I wake to the now comforting and quickly familiar noises and movements of a European express train. Outside there is now a snowswept Polish landscape. There is lots of snow, probably several feet deep in places. Snow was a thing that adventurers encountered on polar expeditions, so it somehow made me feel more purposeful.

A significant milestone in becoming a successful long-range rail traveller is approaching. I need to visit the bathroom. Of course there is no bath (or even a shower on most trains), but it sounds nicer than saying it's time to get comfortable using a cramped communal toilet on a moving train. I pick up my specially devised Swiss Army wash bag (with a built-in hanger) and head out to the end of the carriage, remembering to lock my door on the way. Past the inner door, the carriage floor is covered in fine snow. I pick one of the two toilets at random and peer inside. It looks spotlessly clean. Buttons dispense soap, water and hot air. The WC is operated by a pressure system, like on an aircraft. I go about my business and return happy with my first experience of train-based ablutions on this journey.

On the way back to my compartment I bump into a smartly dressed steward carrying a cup of coffee balanced on a little tray. By process of deduction, this means we must now have a restaurant car. He points me in the right direction (important to know which way when the carriages have been shuffled after you get on) and I practise the correct etiquette for passing other passengers in the narrow corridor. If you were an eskimo you might try to do this face-to-face, but passing back-to-back is more acceptable to the average European. Like fish on a tropical reef, people in the corridor often move back into their compartment to let you pass.

My other bit of training before breakfast was learning how to manage the journey between the carriages. The doors are pneumatic and open for about five seconds when a lever is pulled. Between each of the carriages is a no man's land of steel and ice. All that separates you from the frozen outside world is a flexible rubber tunnel and a metal floor plate that moves as the tracks curve. At my first attempt I thought that I might actually get stuck. Rather alarmingly the first set of doors closed behind me before I could reach over to press the button and open the second set. I was left briefly balancing like a surfer, one foot on each carriage footplate with nothing to hang onto. I will need to practise this manoeuvre some more if I am to become a real train adventurer.

When I reach the restaurant car, four along from my own carriage, I wonder if I have accidentally smoked something in Amsterdam. Is it a dream? If Carlsberg made European restaurant cars, this is what they would produce. A smiling waiter behind the bar counter greets me like he's expecting to see me. He even asks me how I am today, in perfect English. The carriage is functional, but comes very close to feeling like a real café. It has a kind of breakfast bar with high stools down one side and tables laid out for breakfast opposite. There is a digital sign above the door indicating our speed, our temperature and the next stop. At the recommendation of the waiter, I order sausages and scrambled eggs and then find a table. He brings over a freshly brewed coffee and a range of condiments for my breakfast. The food is served on branded china with all the trimmings of a reasonable restaurant. Everything has been freshly cooked, and I vow that if I manage to return safely I will write to my local train operator and let them know about this experience.

We speed past villages of snow-covered wooden cottages with smoking chimneys. Outside on the roads people are busy de-icing their family cars before heading to work. It's definitely getting colder out there as we progress eastwards.

I am about to head back to Carriage 180 when the waiter asks me what I would like to eat for lunch. He offers some suggestions and I consider these options. Rather than a choice of sandwiches, or an all-day breakfast, Chef can apparently make all sorts of things. I'm on the cusp of pre-ordering something tasty when I remember about the small matter of the delay and finding a connection to Moscow. Resigned to a missed feast I politely decline and go back to my own compartment to await further news from our conductor.

She has noticed me in the corridor as I arrive back outside my locked compartment door. She comes to see me, bringing with her a cup of dreadful instant coffee and a stale cheese sandwich, possibly to better prepare me for news of the delay. After a quick chat, as much of a chat as railway English allows, the good news is that she thinks that my connection might still be possible. I'm somewhat sceptical, but welcome the possibility that all is not lost. There will be no sure way of knowing until we reach the connecting station. Maybe she just doesn't want any arguments until we are off her carriage. Before leaving she hands me a PKP form to complete, to get compensation for my late arrival. As it's in Polish,

I have no idea if it's a generous offer or not. All I want to do is catch my next train.

Warsaw actually has three stations very close together, so getting off the sleeper carriage needs to be carefully choreographed. Passengers are marshalled out in the correct order, like parachutists getting ready to leave a cramped aircraft. I will be the last to jump today, so I hang back as we stop first at Warszawa Zachodnia and then the main Warszawa Centralna station. My stop was Warszawa Wschodnia, on the east of the city. I had heard it wasn't one of Poland's most friendly railway stations, and that it was generally full of slightly dodgy people. I hope that I won't be there long enough to meet any of them today.

Getting on and off a train in Europe is quite different from back in the United Kingdom; the carriage floor is higher up and there are two big steps between the level of the carriage and that of the platform. In fact many stations don't have proper platforms, so a gantry of further steps can then be manually dropped to ground level. Gear assembled after the Centralna stop, I'm ready at the outer door for the next stop and the possibility of a train to Moscow. We pull in, and the conductor wishes me good luck before she helps me get the baggage down onto the platform. Holding on to a handle I tentatively try my boot on its surface. It slips wildly, but I manage to hang on. Should I have packed some crampons?

Getting my balance back, I try to look like what is normal to me as a seasoned rail adventurer. The air is much colder now than when I boarded the train in Amsterdam – this gives me a feeling of progress in a measure different from just the distance travelled. I say goodbye to the PKP lady and start to look around to see if there really might still be a train to Moscow, now more than two hours after it should have departed from Warsaw.

I don't have to look very far. The D405, known as the *Vltava*, is still sitting at the platform opposite. It has been held for our arrival. The Basel to Moscow carriage that had caused the delay on my previous train must have been my salvation now, probably being the main reason for the *Vltava* being held until we have arrived. I'm just a lucky bystander from Carriage 181, which stays here in Warsaw until a return journey to Amsterdam later in the day.

Fired up by this, and relieved that I will not be stranded after all, I scuttle down the concrete steps under the platform and climb up on the opposite side. This is an old school station, without modern conveniences like lifts or escalators. Getting used to the ice, I balance over my feet and slide along the platform in search of my new carriage, number 345. I pass by several sleek and modern Russian carriages (built in Austria). They are painted in the corporate grey and red colour scheme of RZD, the state-owned Russian Railway. If only one of these were mine. Next to these is a single Russian carriage painted in the older blue and red colours that date back a couple of decades. At one end is a sign hanging behind a net curtain in the window proclaiming it to be Carriage 345. Bugger.

At first no one seems very interested in me as I load my gear up onto the Russian wagon, but eventually a rather casually dressed tall blonde conductor (known as the *provodnitsa*) appears to see what the noise is about. Once she has inspected my paperwork (all in order again!) she shows me to my compartment, which is right next to her own at one end of the coach. Looking into her place as we walk past, my first impressions are that they look like the radio room of a Russian submarine. All the space seems to lack is an Enigma machine. She tells me that her name is Olga. Breaking the Russian stereotype, she smiles a lot, but speaks no English. As I speak no Russian, we communicate purely by international sign language.

Looking into my own compartment, my heart sinks a bit. I have obviously drawn the short straw with this carriage – it has the shabby chic look of the Cold War, with beaten-up wooden furnishings, flowery fabrics and lace curtains. Using every available space, I stow my bags and sit down in the single chair opposite my bunk. Trying to think positively, if this were a Soviet submarine, I would be in the captain's cabin. Despite the state of the carriage I can't help but feel happy, though. This is a train like no other I have ever been on, and I'm seriously excited about the journey ahead. Olga brings me a cup of tea in one of those traditional Russian glasses with an ornate metal outer cup and handle. I decide to take a moment to practise my Sean Connery Russian accent. Connery played a totally unconvincing Soviet naval officer in the film *The Hunt for Red October*. Nevertheless, the film still became one of the biggest grossing films of 1990.

Back in the real world, I'm not prepared for what happens next. The waiter from the EN447 train appears on our platform carrying a covered tray, and proceeds to climb on board the carriage. He grins at me from the corridor, and before I can say anything, serves me pork schnitzel, potatoes and sauerkraut together with a cold bottle of Zywiec beer at my submarine-sized cabin table. Unbelievable. So good I wonder if I'm dreaming again. I tip him and thank him profusely. He must have worked out at breakfast that I was headed to Moscow and the *Vltava* has no restaurant on board. Olga didn't say anything, so I wondered if this might actually be a regular occurrence – a way to use leftover food and earn some tips. I really don't care though; it's both enterprising and socially uplifting. Up until that moment I have been so uptight about being conned by people. I have drilled myself to trust no one as my first instinct. But my heart now melts and I instantly became a huge fan of Poland, Polish people and PKP. Marvellous.

There is something exciting about setting off on a Russian train for the very first time. The setup feels so different from European trains. Everything seems calm, and no one looks at all surprised or bothered that we are running a couple of hours late. Most people leave their compartment doors open, play music and chat with each other. It is a nice atmosphere, and just what I had hoped for. Perhaps the secret to this is that people seem to have really settled in. They are dressed comfortably, and no one seems to care how they might look to others. I had heard about the Russian train dress code – shorts and flip-flops are on the smart end of the scale in first class. At first it feels inherently wrong to be wearing a pair of shorts on board a train when outside it's well below freezing, but I quickly get used to it. The trick will be remembering to change before leaving the train.

Carriage 345 is fairly conventional in the sense that it still has a corridor and ten compartments. At one end are two bathrooms, and at the other Olga and her radio room. Russian train design seems to dictate that there are lots of uncovered pipes and valves, as if to signal that the design might have been drawn up in a submarine yard somewhere on the North Cape. The corridor is not as narrow as the Polish train, I think because overall the carriages are a bit wider. On the corridor floor there is a long dirty blanket from one end to the other, protecting the carpet from the snow- and salt-covered boots of arriving passengers. Mobile devices are suspended from every horizontal surface, daisy-chained off the two power sockets intended only for use by Olga and her vacuum cleaner. I also spot some power cables routed under the carpet to a few of the compartments, allowing movies to be watched on laptops and the long-range texting to loved ones.

I haven't been looking at my watch, and I forget we are still in Warsaw whilst the Basel carriage is shunted round. I'm reminded of this, though, when with a gentle tug from the locomotive we slowly accelerate in the direction of Minsk. Olga stops by to have a look at my passport and make a note of its number. I hope I'm not going to be singled out for special treatment at the border with Belarus.

The journey today seems much smoother than last night. I think the reason for this is that the line is straight and the landscape totally flat. Poland stretches on and on during the afternoon. In a massive rail cliché I play some mood music and stare out at the wintry countryside. Trying to match my music with my location, I play Kraftwerk and the seminal *Trans-Europe Express* album. Ralf Hutter has just the right lyric for my predicament – 'Europe, endless'.

The atmosphere changes rather quickly as the sun sinks behind the icy treeline. Olga has put her uniform on and is clearly preparing for the approaching frontier. To signal the commencement of border games, she turns on the overhead lights and moves up and down the corridor opening all the doors. She gives it to me in a single word, 'customs'. We reach Brest on the Polish border at about 17:00 and begin a process that is alien to me. As we sit next to a sterile platform surrounded by razor-wire-topped fencing, paperwork is handed out and passports are checked in microscopic detail. It feels a bit odd, as I don't need to go anywhere, queue up or do anything other than complete the forms. Everyone comes to see me, and my compartment is rather too popular a place tonight, as I am the only non-Russian passport holder in our carriage.

After the train has been searched by armed police with dogs, we say goodbye to the Polish security services and are pulled very slowly across a big metal bridge that is guarded on both sides by men with assault rifles and even more menacing-looking dogs. This is totally Cold War. On the other side of is Terespol and the Belarus frontier, and on the platform there waiting to meet us is a whole delegation of assorted officials.

They march up and down the platform a bit (I assume to keep warm) before climbing onto their allotted carriages.

They don't seem very friendly, but as I am to learn that this is the Russian military way. Some of them fail to hide their surprise when they discover that they have a decadent Westerner in Compartment 9 of Carriage 345, once belonging to the CCCP. It might have been my state of mind, but the Russian army sergeant who searches my compartment looks strangely alluring to me. She has definitely been trained not to smile, but you can just imagine that after a hard day's work (and a maybe a glass of vodka), she would also enjoy a good night out. The male soldiers are mainly miserable and just try to look as hard and intimidating as possible. My passport and declaration papers are taken away for a more detailed inspection, so all that I can do is sit back and wait hopefully for their return.

With no other formal duties to perform I swap text messages with friends. Today is Black Friday, the night when everyone is out at their office Christmas parties. I see pictures of mildly inebriated people sat at tables festooned with crackers and a reasonable selection of wine. Although I don't much like Christmas parties, tonight I'm rather missing their comfort and familiarity. By comparison I am very much alone and in a hostile environment. I can hear more slamming of doors and then the sound of boots purposefully march-ing towards my compartment. An immigration officer appears and steps in. He is a captain, and he wears a long tailored trench coat and carries an expensive-looking brown leather briefcase. I won-der if this is an officially issued item, or possibly a gift from a rich oligarch uncle. He completes his look with some hexagonal wire-rimmed glasses, rather like the Russian villain from the 1980s James Bond classic film *For Your Eyes Only*.

His body language immediately gives me the impression that there might be a problem, so I stand up, which I feel is the best thing I can do to show respect. I'm still unused to people coming to visit me rather than the other way around. I wait for him to pronounce judgement on my application to enter Belarus, but he says nothing. Then I wait some more. He just keeps staring, saying nothing. His eyes are boring a hole into my very soul. Needing desperately to fill the void, I can't stop myself, so I ask him rather too casu-ally 'All good …?'

He then starts to tap my passport in his other hand, as if he can't decide what to do with me. Is this the moment that some sort of donation might be needed? Or is he just making his final immigration decision based upon his instinct? Maybe he has some X-ray superpower developed behind the Iron Curtain. I'm taken by surprise as he thrusts his arm forward, as if it were an immigration drill manoeuvre. In his hand is my passport, together with a stamped immigration card and transit visa for Belarus. My papers are in order! The icing on the cake is a curt salute before he turns and marches back down the corridor. I can only assume he had just been practising his interrogation technique on me, as the papers had obviously been stamped before he returned to the train.

Before we leave Terespol there is one more job to complete. It is a task that the average rail travelling European would find utterly bizarre. We are going to change the wheels of each carriage of the train. Russia has a wider gauge of track than in western Europe, so the solution for international trains is not to change into a new set of carriages, but to literally swap the wheels (if you are a train person, I apologise; it is of course actually the bogies that are changed). So we are shunted into a shed, carriage by carriage, and lifted up by massive hydraulic machines. Oily men with big hammers work underneath us whilst life goes on pretty much as normal inside the carriage – apart from the toilets being locked. From what I can see outside there is little health and safety to worry about here. It is work for manly men, who at best wear a reflective vest to protect them from the swinging hooks on the gantries overhead. Hard hats are clearly regarded as unnecessary as long as you have a lit cigarette to keep you safe.

The transformation to Russian five-foot gauge takes about an hour, and as soon as our carriage has been lowered and shunted back to the rest of the train, a crowd of babushkas selling food and drink arrive to take advantage of our lack of restaurant car. They sell their wares door to door, and are quite excitable. Out of big bags come bundles of home-cooked food wrapped in Russian newspaper. I buy a couple of beers and some rather good cheese-stuffed blinis. I'm sure I'll be paying more than anyone else on the train, but I have no idea what the street price for a cheese blini might be. Casting an eye over the newspaper, I see that the crossword puzzle has already been completed.

After some tooting of the horn we move off again, now in the direction of Minsk. Our border crossing has taken more than three hours, and it's been educational to me as a trainee rail adventurer. Examining my freshly stamped transit visa for Belarus and my exit card, I assume that I need to hand this over at the Russian border. When will that be? I consult my handwritten notes and copied sheets of timetables from my folder. It looks to me that we will cross into the Russian Federation in the early hours of tomorrow morning – so it'll be another night with little sleep. I decide to try my hand at some more international sign language with Olga to confirm this timing.

She seems to have gone a bit native now we have crossed the border, and sits in her compartment dressed in her pyjamas drinking tea. She tries her best to interpret my stamping motions, waving my passport in one hand and the exit card in the other hand. She gestures that I should relax and that everything is okay, but don't think she understands my question. I give up, and rather kindly she decides to take me to see some passengers in a compartment towards the middle of the carriage.

In Compartment 6 I'm the centre of attention, as the assembled group of worldly wise Russians stare at my strange passport and wonder what I might be trying to ask. Eventually they get it and there is pointing with fingers at a timetable. It turns out that in immigration terms Belarus is treated as being part of Russia, so there will be no further border formalities tonight. My exit card will be good as far as the Mongolian border, where I say goodbye to Mother Russia. I thank them all, repeating over and over my only useful word of Russian: '*Spasiba!*' I really wish I had bothered to learn some more of the language. All I have is a clever picture book. This allows me to point to pictures of things like strange fruit and riot policemen. I also have an app on my phone, but it seems to focus on phrases needed for the Russian dating scene. It didn't have anything on exit cards, but did have phrases like 'I love you very much' and 'Let's get married in the morning'. It says them out loud on my phone in a creepy accent: to my untrained ear, 'I love you' sounds something like 'yellow lorry, blue lorry'.

I settled down for the night in my compartment and recheck my plans for arriving in Moscow. I was getting ready for a TV dinner of beer, blinis and a movie on my iPad, when a chap from a compartment down the carriage pops his head round the door. He smiles and asks me if I know Wayne Rooney. This is my travel Achilles heel, as I never know how to handle football-related conversations with foreigners. I actually don't care much for the beautiful game, but football talk seems to help travellers across the world engage with local people. I decide to bluff my way through this one. I reply simply 'Manchester United!' quite loudly and with some excitement, hoping I haven't made a hideous schoolboy error. I must have passed the test, as he gestures that I should follow him and join the occupants of his compartment for a drink. I smile and wave at him like he might be a madman with an axe, and he heads off without me. On reflection, it's me who would be the madman to pass up on the chance to meet friendly fellow travellers. This was what travel by train is supposed to be all about, so I pick up my bottle of Scotch and quickly head after him.

At the far end of the carriage live what I

discover to be two Moldovan car salesmen returning from a business trip to Warsaw. A girl from the compartment next door, who speaks a tiny bit of English, has also joined us. Olga looks in from the corridor, perhaps concerned that I am being led astray. The Moldovans prefer their cheap and not very smooth 'French' brandy to my Scotch, but I try not to hold that against them. We feast on salted boiled potatoes and onions. The sharing of food seems to be a key element of the endless toasts. It is going to be almost impossible to leave before we run out of brandy. When, much much later, I finally excuse myself, it is explained to me that you can't go to bed without a fresh round of toasts and/or finishing the current bottle. Not being one to create a poor impression of Great Britain, I follow these drinking laws until the brandy is no more. Our final toast is to Mir. I thought it was a bit unusual to toast a space station, but later found out it's the Russian word for 'friendship'.

I'm left that night with one more duty to perform before retiring. I have to make up my bed. With hindsight I should have considered doing this before the Moldovan drinks bash. I have to be honest and say it doesn't go very well. For some reason I decide to sleep on a berth above my seat, and all I manage to do is to it get it stuck at a rather unnatural angle on top of the lower berth, the vital bracket falling off completely at one end. Seeking help from my new Moldovan friends, we struggle with it in the style of three drunks putting up a tent for the first time. Eventually I have a bed. Before finally turning in I decide to go for a short stroll with my camera. Olga spots me going through the door at the end of the carriage and is perhaps worried about the possibility of me getting lost or even jumping off the train. She puts an arm round me and gently steers me back into my billet. I must have drunk more brandy than I should have.

Day Five, Smolensk, Russian Federation
Distance travelled so far: 3,250 km

Moscow time (GMT+3)

Station	Arrival	Departure
Warsaw		12:35
Moscow, next day	11:53	

Several hours later, I wake shivering and with a rather thick head. There is a lot of banging going on in the corridor. It is daylight outside, but I have forgotten to account for the two-hour time zone shift overnight. Once out of my slightly broken bed, I organise my things into a tidy pile at one end, then set about making some home-brewed coffee. When I emerge from my compartment to get some hot water I'm confronted by a Russian Mr Fix It chap, clad in oily blue overalls. He has a big leather bag of spanners, but by far his favourite tool is his trusty lump hammer. With careful precision he taps every pipe, as if he can deduce the source of any problem by noise alone. Olga is supervising, still dressed in her Russian railway pyjamas. She puts the kettle on for me, and with a bit of sign language explains that our boiler has stopped working, and she apologises that it's so cold.

The Moldovans are rather sensibly still in bed, so I take the time to prepare for any further football-related questions whilst sipping my first cup of coffee. In the background the frozen fields of Smolensk whizz past. I remember a good football saying, and try to commit it memory for later on – 'The thing about Arsenal is that they always try to walk it in'.

I would have been quite happy to sit here for the rest of the morning, but my bowels indicate in a very firm way that they won't wait until we reach Moscow, and I have to endure what is a pretty rough trip to the single toilet at the end of our carriage. In keeping with the submarine look, none of the pipework is hidden. There are a confusing series of levers and knobs with instructions in Russian to control the mad plumbing. I suspect that it has not been cleaned properly since the fall of the Berlin Wall.

With the rising sun, snow melts from the branches of the trees on the embankments and gets flung all over the carriage as we hurtle along. The atmosphere on board is a little like the last day of term at boarding school. Passengers pack up their belongings and, I'm guessing, chat about their plans for what they hope to do in Moscow. Small towns became suburbs, and before long we are in the vast urban sprawl of the outskirts of the capital city of the Russian Federation. I was expecting to see the huge brutalist-style apartment blocks, but no one had told me about the amazing gothic Stalinist skyscrapers. With the backdrop of bright blue winter sky, the city looks amazing. My first impression is that it is much larger and more European-looking than I had imagined it would be.

Our track joins dozens of others carrying hundreds of trains in and out of the western side of the city. Eventually we slow down and pull into Moskva Belorusskaya station. Olga, now wearing something more suitable, opens the carriage doors for the final time. Outside the air is freezing and the platform covered in an invisible coating of ultra-slippery ice. Like a scene in a disaster movie, passengers reach out and grab each other's hands in an attempt to get off without falling over. I say my goodbyes to Olga and the Moldovans, but continue to wait near our carriage, as I have arranged for someone to meet me off the train. Still waiting after about 20 minutes I'm losing the feeling in my feet, and decide that I need to press on by myself. I had been hoping to recreate a scene from a Cold War spy thriller by greeting my contact with a line like 'In Moscow the rivers are bright blue in the winter'. I shall just have to save this line for next time.

Waving goodbye once more to Olga, I toboggan my luggage along the platform towards the station building. This is my first time in a Russian station. It looks like any other station, apart from the way it is painted in an unusual shade of traditional Russian railway green. There are a few touts hanging about, and I pick the least dangerous-looking one to reveal my secret that I have need of his services. He wears a thick sheepskin coat and a black leather cap, and has clearly seen me coming. I show him an address and he says he knows where I'm going, it's a long way away, and that it's going to cost me 'Tih-see-chuh' rubles. I don't know how many that is, but am in no position to effectively negotiate.

Some 20 minutes later (10 minutes to defrost the windows) we are pulling out of the deeply frozen car park in a clapped-out Lada, driven by a big man with limited interest in the Russian highway code. It takes a while to get to my hotel in Sokolniki, a suburb to the north-east of the city. It turns out 'Tih-see-chuh' is a thousand, so I dip into my wallet and find a fresh banknote for the driver. That works out at £15 for a 45-minute game of *Grand Theft Auto, Downtown Moscow*. Thinking about it, this could have been worse.

Six: Firefox

Day Six, Moscow, Russian Federation
Distance travelled so far: 3,692 km

When I was planning my trip, I worked out that most hotels in Moscow fell into one of three categories. The first were hotels that were a hangover from the days of the communist regime. These had no mod cons, but instead freestanding fridges, old school telephones and presumably lots of bugs (not of the insect variety). Second were the new five star central hotels for seriously rich tourists and businessmen. These were all polished brass and chandeliers – luxury, but aimed at oligarchs and ruble billionaires. That left the third option, the modern suburban business hotels for travellers on some form of budget. I had chosen one of these, the theory being that after a few days sleeping on various trains it would feel quite luxurious. It turned out that I was spot on.

I could almost be checking into a business chain hotel anywhere in the world. The staff are young and multilingual. There are no suspicious stares at an arriving capitalist. The only new process I need to perform here is to ask the hotel to formally register my visa with the local authorities (a requirement for stays of more than seven days, but I'm taking no chances with local militia). Technically a visa needs reregistering in each city you stay in, but once out of Moscow I'll be too mobile to have to worry about this requirement. With this done, I shower and decide I need at least an hour's rest before I tackle anything more.

Several hours later, outside my hotel in the darkness, I wander about in the snow feeling like an extra from the 1983 thriller *Gorky Park*. Although this was filmed in Helsinki and Stockholm, it is a film that makes me imagine what life as a Muscovite in the Soviet era might have really been like. In the park today, people cruise past me on ice skates in all directions and crowd into wooden bars selling mulled wine and sugary little cakes. I'm not sure how safe it is, but I hope that the anonymity of darkness helps disguise my identity as a traveller rather than a local. Everyone seems to be having a good time, or as much of a good time as it's possible to have in the freezing darkness of a moderately unfashionable Moscow suburb.

I find the shop signs deeply confusing. Not only are they in the almost unintelligible Cyrillic alphabet, but also their design and style is misleading. I first visit a bar that turns out to be a hairdresser, and then a restaurant that is in fact a pet shop. On the brink of giving up and going back to my hotel, I find an Uzbek restaurant that really is an Uzbek restaurant, and treat myself to a feast of pilaf, grilled meats and freshly baked bread. Around me, Russians smoke heavily, drink tea and look a bit less miserable than perhaps is normal.

After dinner I have to hurry back to my hotel. I'm underdressed for the conditions, and the chill cuts right through my thin trousers. The pedestrian crossing on the busy road outside my hotel makes me wait an agonising 90 seconds before turning green. This is almost enough time to lose circulation were you to stop moving. The staff at Reception seem to take little interest in me as I walk back in, and I briefly wonder if my room might be bugged. I decide that the activities of the typical guest staying here are unlikely to be worth much to the FSB (the current name for the KGB), but following Roger Moore's lead (without a special hairbrush that turns into a bug detector), I inspect all the light switches, buttons and telephones in my room for listening devices before settling down for the night. Once again my sleep is punctuated with nightmares of missing trains and being arrested for having the wrong paperwork.

The following morning, the sun rises later than I'm used to for the time of day. Outside huge queues of dirty-snow-covered cars make slow progress along the icy streets. I sit in a huge and mainly empty hotel restaurant drinking instant coffee whilst working out my plans. I have a couple of days to see the sights of Moscow before I am due to join the weekly Trans-Mongolian service to Beijing, departing late on Tuesday evening.

I decide to give up using risky unlicensed taxi-cabs, and instead become a self-taught user of the Moscow metro system. Once I have worked out how the ticketing works and have overcome my fear of the violent turnstiles (if your ticket is not in order they snap closed, trapping you, or if you're really unlucky cutting you in two), I descend into the subterranean world. To begin with I use colours and shapes to recognise my stops, occasionally admitting defeat and getting help from anyone who has time to point me in the right direction. I have no shame here; I'm past the very British male habit of being too embarrassed to ask for directions. The stations are stunning, each decorated in a unique style celebrating an aspect of past Soviet achievement. One station can have several different names, one for each line, and if you can't read the Cyrillic alphabet, it's a bit of an adventure at first. The strange thing is that after a bit of staring at Cyrillic, it is possible to start to see what the word might say. It's a bit hit and miss at first, but I think if I stayed here for a few weeks I would eventually work it out.

Up on the surface I visit tourist attractions, and even find time for some light shopping. At one local weekend market I find a suitable *ushanka* for the climate. It is the sort that all Russian soldiers and sailors wear, made of fur. Sean Connery wears one, too, in *The Hunt for Red October*, but his is the naval officer's version, made of lambswool. Other than hats, the market is packed with things that would put most European customs officers into a stress-related condition. Amidst all the wooden dolls and kitsch Soviet-era junk there are flick knives, bayonets, pistols, and even ageing assault rifles. The only other thing that I decide to buy is a small icon painting, to bring me luck in my adventures.

During my stay in Moscow I make an important, and as it turns out lifelong, new friend. His name is Alexey, and he is my fixer. Alexey is a short, rather stocky Russian in his early 40s who has devoted his post-army-conscript life to looking after visitors like me with strange requests. He is by far the most sincere Russian I have ever met, and he immediately takes personal responsibility for my personal wellbeing in a disarmingly unRussian way – Be careful of this, be careful of that, Have you got your hat? Do you need to visit the bathroom?

So now I have my very own Passepartout. He always wears a parka jacket and woollen beany cap, even in heated buildings. He keeps detailed notes of his clients in a small black book, and has a phone that can access the internet, but for some reason he has no email address. Serious and thoughtful, at first he kept his humour hidden from me, but after a trip to the Central Armed Forces Museum, I discover that what makes him laugh out loud is a bit of a niche subject – the ineptitude of the Chechen militia. I have no idea why; it must be an ex-soldier thing.

Day Seven, Monino, Russian Federation
Distance travelled so far: 3,692 km

Before leaving home I had decided to invest a day, and a large pile of rubles, visiting a little-known airfield a couple of hours outside Moscow. It's called the Gagarin Air Force Academy, now home to the Central Air Force Museum. Now, with special permissions achieved and background checks done, I'm going to get to see what was until recently a closed place to foreigners, a place packed with previously classified state secrets.

When we set off in the morning, it's still dark.

With a private car and a driver, we slither through the snow and work our way through the commuter traffic outside Moscow. Topics of conversation with Alexey are always interesting: politics, religion, law and order, big game hunting, even art. The thought crosses my mind that actually he's an undercover FSB agent. That would be clever. After an hour we turn off the main road and drive through a quiet and nondescript suburban town called Monino. It doesn't look very secret – rather, just a dull dormitory town – but it's a Russian technique to put secret things in places that you don't expect to find them. Leaving the car in a residential drive, we head on foot along a very frozen road. My progress is slow, as the last thing I want to do today is fall over and break an ankle. After about a half a mile we arrive at a security point, behind which I can hear dogs barking.

We check in at a drab reception building that looks nothing like an air force base. Alexey and I are introduced to our appointed Russian Air Force guide for the day, a lady called Natalia. The experience is at first is a bit strained. The staff are not very comfortable letting foreigners inside to steal the secrets of their exotic flying machines. It seems to all be about approach. Whenever I ask a difficult question, or to inspect something covered up, at first it's just not possible. A bit of a chat from Alexey later, this becomes maybe, and before long it's no problem at all, but 'just for me'. I think these people simply need to feel that they are still in control. There is actually never any doubt of this, as I have seen the size of their guard dogs.

In 1982 Clint Eastwood directed and starred in a film about stealing the most secret plane from the CCCP, codename Firefox. The plane was fictional, but based on the massive worries that the West had about the Soviet breakthroughs in aviation technology in the later part of the Cold War. I was about to see why for myself.

Outside the warmth of the hangar there is a whole airfield to explore – nearly 200 planes set out in long lines, like a grand Soviet parade. Today I'm acting as the general. We inspect lines of scary aircraft, each with a number and a NATO codeword – fighters like the Frogfoot, Fiddler and Fantail, bombers like the Bison, Bear, Blinder and Backfire. Natalia talks to us like we're shopping in a military supermarket, and she would make an excellent arms dealer: 'You want the high-altitude version? The one with the 150-kiloton warhead? No problem – it's just along here.'

Of course I can't understand anything she says – Alexey is there to translate, which he does in a very matter-of-fact way. Whilst they chat to each other about weapons yields, bomber ranges and the issues of high-G manoeuvrability, I stand rather dumbfounded in front of each of the monstrous bombers. They look like modern sci-fi fantasies. What is melting my mind is the fact that many were flying in the skies of the CCCP in the 1950s. I make the mistake of asking to have my photograph taken with one aircraft that is particularly unusual. It's a MiG-105 spaceplane prototype. My mistake is not the security issue of taking a photograph of a plane that did not officially exist until the 1990s, but in under-estimating the depth of the snow that it's sitting in. I am quickly up to my waist, but I pretend I don't mind, and carry on struggling towards it. Natalia briefly stops talking about transonic turbojet performance whilst Alexey takes the picture. Back on the path I dust myself off and we carry on, turning our attention to the excellent Soviet safety record of transporting nuclear bombs in huge Mil helicopters.

Day Eight, Moscow, Russian Federation
Distance travelled so far: 3,692 km

It's time to get back on the rails. My final day in Moscow is a busy one, but at Alexey's suggestion I still find time to visit the Tretyakov gallery. I can take or leave the thousands of Orthodox icons, but I become transfixed by the huge and detailed battle paintings by an artist I have never heard of before, Vasily Vereshchagin. Alexey isn't surprised. He likes them too, and suggests that Vereshchagin and I have a lot in common. He explains that we are both gentleman who are heading east to discover new places and write about our adventures. I rather like that, as it makes me feel that bit more of a genuine adventurer than a tourist.

Before checking out of my hotel, I go shopping at a local supermarket. I'm not sure what's going to be on sale in a Russian supermarket, but my images of Soviet food shortages are out the window. It's a modern shop that sells nearly everything. There are particularly impressive collections of coffee, chocolates and vodka. In 1960s home economics parlance, you might describe this as my 'big shop'; I manage to fill three bags with noodles, tins of meat, porridge, cheese, crackers, preserved sausage – and vitally, some cartons of reasonable-looking Spanish wine. I have to confess that I can't work out what some of tins actually contain. Animal? Probably, but which ones I'm not so sure. The noodles are easy, though, as they have pictures of some amazing gourmet dishes printed on the outsides of the plastic pots. I end up with more than I can carry, but I'm not so worried as Alexey is actually coming with me to find my next train. I only wish he could come further with me on this journey, as he's a top chap.

One of my worst nightmares has been missing

the train, and for a moment today this fear nearly turns into reality. The early evening is spent crawling along very, very slowly in a huge rush-hour traffic jam. Fortunately, though, I have a secret weapon. He is my driver, and his name is Victor. Heavily influenced by *The French Connection*, he dresses like an extra from the film and drives like he is performing an elaborate stunt sequence to camera for a new film in the franchise, this time set in downtown Moscow. He shows no fear of pushing us through seemingly impassable jammed side streets. When the going gets tough he just pulls his leather cap down an extra inch and grins. It's a slightly insane smile, and I think Alexey might have been goading him on a bit. When we finally pull up outside Yaroslavsky station we still have, to my amazement, 30 minutes to spare. Victor smiles even more wildly as we get out the now smoking car. It distinctly smells like it might need an oil and clutch change. I thank him and give him a big tip, and this is returned by a beaming and non-Russian smile. He tells Alexey that I should be careful out there in Siberia. Almost like Siberia makes Moscow look like a very safe place. The hidden friendliness and kindness of Russian people has been one of my biggest surprises so far on this adventure.

Yaroslavsky station is in the east of Moscow, and is the departure point for all trains heading towards Siberia. It's not as glamorous as Leningrad station next door. (This is rather like comparing Euston and St Pancras stations in London.) Once past security and inside Yaroslavsky, there is little for us to do other than sit and wait for a platform announcement. For the first time in ages I am not alone in having lots of bags. Soldiers, traders and family groups surround me. They look like they have all their worldly possessions with them, packed in blue and red striped plastic woven bags – the sort of bag you see on airport luggage reclaim belts across Asia.

Having a Passepartout here is much more than just about someone to help carry some of my bags. Whilst I guard the bags and fend off the drunks, Alexey is able to perform a close target reconnaissance of where he thinks the train might depart from. I'm sure the Russian army have their own name for this, but we don't discuss military tactics very much. Having a Russian speaker with me also allows decryption of the Cyrillic departures board. Alexey is back from his recce and he says he has found both the platform and the train. We gather up the bags and head outside into the snow and ice. When I lift my big duffel bag I'm alarmed to discover that its relative warmth and privacy has become home to a whole community of big cockroaches in just the few minutes it has been on the station floor.

We trudge round the outside of the station

through the snow towards a hidden international platform. Over the public address system a woman announces all the departures in Russian. It could be the weather forecast or the results of today's ice hockey games for all I understand. Each announcement is accompanied by a little musical jingle that I will get to know very well in the days ahead. I'm sure it has been composed to keep the locals as happy as possible in this climate. There is something else too. In the air I can smell burning coal. Do they still have steam trains?

As we approach Platform 3, in the darkness I get my first glimpse of Train 004. It looks a little past its prime and is painted in a dull-looking green colour. Smartly dressed Chinese guards are standing to attention at the end of each carriage, awaiting their passengers. As Alexey and I walk down the platform I begin to notice that not all the carriages are actually the same. At the back of the train there are some different-coloured old Russian carriages, next to these a restaurant car, and then ten identical green Chinese coaches. Towards the back end of these is Carriage no 9, my new home. It is obvious that no one will be getting on unless their paperwork is in order. The guard scrutinises my tickets very carefully, as dirty smoke wafts past us from a chimney at the end of the carriage – a coal-burning fire to heat the compartments and make hot water.

It dawns on me that whilst Passepartout can speak German, Russian and Spanish, he doesn't speak a word of Chinese. The bad news is that this is a Chinese train, and they speak no Russian. This is a bit of a disappointment, as I had got used to using Alexey as my universal translator. The guard studies the detail of my international ticket to 'Peking' for some time. Then in a very non-Russian way, he smiles at me, the way Chinese smile at most things when you don't know if they are sad, happy, angry or just indifferent to the situation. I'm a bona fide passenger, and allowed to board the Trans-Mongolian train. They even let Alexey on too.

I don't know it at the time, but I am in fact to be the only passenger in Carriage no 9 that night, as the guards want to complete their paperwork as soon as I am on board. Entering the carriage for the first time, I am struck immediately by the aroma. It has a unique smell. A hint of cat mixed with furniture polish, together with some long-dead fish in the background. I hope I'll get used to it. Going against everything I have been told, the carriage is cold inside. One of the guards shows me to my compartment. It is right in the centre of the carriage. I had asked my Russian agent if this would be possible, as I had heard it is smoother in the middle, plus I would be as far away as possible from both the smokers and the toilets. I dump the luggage onto my bed (the only real space) and say farewell to Alexey. What a thoroughly nice man, and absolute proof that Russians can be caring, funny and wise. I'm sure that I will really miss him in the days ahead.

The two guards in my carriage, Mr Li and Mr Chen, have very distinctive personalities and different unofficial jobs on board. Li is the happy one and perhaps most interested in my personal welfare. He does most of the getting off at stops and associated passenger paperwork. When he isn't doing these things he is also the resident chef in our carriage. The Chinese staff are self-caterers, preferring to make their own meals rather than visit the Russian restaurant car. Chen is a bit younger and thinner, and looks a bit less happy at having to deal with passengers, especially Westerners like me. His main responsibility is keeping the fire burning, restocking the carriage with coal twice a day and – hopefully after washing his hands – managing other on-board supplies like blankets and linen. Neither of them seems to feel they have any responsibility for actually cleaning our carriage, so I take on this role myself, as the only passenger.

Before we set off, Mr Chen arrives at my compartment with some bedding, and Mr Li stops by to collect some more details about my strange red passport. He doesn't seem very convinced about the existence of the United Kingdom, but he understands that I am from a place called

England. I don't try to confuse him further by explaining that I actually now live in another country called Scotland.

At 21:35 Moscow time, patriotic Russian music is played over the public address system on the platform, and we start to trundle out of the station. It isn't the smooth sensation I have been hoping for. We lurch, jump and then stop as if the train is still attached to something solid. I have to hold onto the bed to steady myself. Meanwhile in the corridor a man with spanners and a long metal probe starts work on a plumbing problem that until this moment I've been blissfully unaware of. The carriage has been lying in frozen idle for a day or two, and the water pipes and the drains are frozen solid. My shower and sink are completely useless unless this can be fixed. Worse than that, it makes the carriage liable to flooding if any tap is left on.

With nothing much else to do, I make my bed and try to settle in by unpacking a few things to make the place a bit more homely. My compartment has two bunks, and I decide that I'm going to sleep in the top bunk so I won't have to pack my bed away each morning – the bottom berth will be my living accommodation, with my bags mostly wedged underneath. Getting up into my bed the first time is an experience: with two steps and a handle at one end, it's more like ascending the turret of a main battle tank than getting into bed. I'll need to practise this man-oeuvre until I can do it in the dark without killing myself.

Opening a can of warm Russian beer that I have picked up in the station, I carefully time my sips to the lurching rhythm of the train. Our next stop will be Nizhni Novgorod in the middle of the night, then Kirov tomorrow morning. I have heard only bad things about Nizhni Novgorod, so I double-lock my door and decide to turn in for the night. I leave the window blind open and stare out into the blackness for a few minutes whilst getting used to the sounds and smells of the train. What look at first like meteors flash past from time to time – burning embers from the fire, or burning bits of carriage if we are on fire?

Seven: The Loneliness of the Long-Distance Rail Traveller

Day Nine, Kirov, Russian Federation
Distance travelled so far: 4,207 km

Moscow time (GMT+3)

Station	Arrival	Stop	Departure
Vladimir	00:30	23	00:53
Nizhni Novgorod	03:40	12	03:52
Kirov	09:44	15	09:59
Balezino	13:27	23	13:50
Perm II	17:30	20	17:50
Yekaterinburg	23:10	23	23:33

I seem to sleep quite well on my first night on the Trans-Mongolian. My bed is wide and covered in a thick pad that looks like it's stuffed with horse-hair. The sheets are pressed clean linen, and after a minor negotiation I claim rights to the extra pillows for the unused berth in my compartment.

Mr Chen isn't keen at first to let me have more pillowcases, but my charm offensive finally pays off.

As we draw into Kirov I prepare for my first ever Trans-Siberian stop. I felt as if I might actually be getting set for a landing on the moon. Boots – check: jumper – check: fleece jacket – check: hat – check: gloves – check. I can see a digital clock on the platform through the mist – 09:52, -21°C. Things are already starting to get pretty chilly. The train comes to a rather lumpy and abrupt halt on Platform 1. The routine is that Mr Li lowers the metal steps then de-ices them with his chisel and sweeps the snow away with a broom before any passengers can dismount. A quick point at the watch and sharing of finger gestures, and that's how long you have in the outside world.

I want to take a photograph of the engine (note to self – get help, have become a trainspotter?) so I plod up the snow-covered platform. I get about ten paces before falling over in a mini snowdrift hiding black ice. My rail adventurer credibility is more damaged than I am, and I get up trying to look as unperturbed by this experience as possible. Some soldiers stare in my direction, but at least they are not laughing out loud. I press on in the direction of the engine.

I can't actually see the locomotive until I get much closer, as the station is shrouded in thick freezing fog. I try to stay in visual range of Mr Li, who isn't keen to lose me on his first stop of the day, but he soon vanishes behind me in the whiteout conditions. It takes about 5 minutes to reach the engine and I feel very alone up front – until the coal truck arrives. A tractor pulls a trailer, which stops at each carriage, where the guard (Mr Chen on Carriage no 9) receives the coal. It gets shovelled onto the floor of the carriage in heaps by men standing in the trailer. The good news is that you can judge how long is left before the train is going to depart by how many of the fourteen carriages are still to be resupplied. So the position of the tractor on the platform is like a giant linear countdown clock.

There isn't too much to see on the station platform, which is a disappointment, as I had hoped to meet more people on my first ever stop. My research has told me that Kirov is located just to the west of the Ural Mountains, the entry point to Siberia when heading east. I read from *Pravda* that it had the highest incidence of twins in the world, and also an unnatural proportion of people with red hair. But today everyone I see is too well wrapped up for me to guess the colour of their hair.

After a few minutes taking arty pictures of the train and its manly driver, I wander back to the relative safety of being right outside Carriage no 9. It would be a good time to smoke – but I don't smoke – so instead I content myself by stamping my feet and watching Chen and Li at work. I think about how I might get back on the train if I were actually ever in that situation of it starting to leave without me. The problem is that you cannot just open the door from the outside. It is not locked, but is too high up to reach, as the stairs have to be lowered from above. I don't fancy my chances. Which would I choose: losing my luggage and staying on the platform, or hanging on to the outside of the moving train? I conclude that the latter would probably result in death by frostbite in a matter of minutes, so I would have to be prepared to stay behind. The most practical learning from this is that whenever I leave the train I need to always be dressed properly and carry my documents with me.

Back on board and in the warmth once again, it feels good to have made my first stop – a minor Trans-Siberian rite of passage. Like some sort of new boy test, apart from the falling-over incident, I feel qualified on the basics of platform protocols and survival. Next time we stop I'll add a few more tasks, like maybe finding a shop. But with no further stops for a few hours I now have some time to explore my surroundings.

Carriage 9 is what the Chinese call soft class. It consists of ten compartments, each with two berths one above the other, and a single chair on the other side of a small table. A small shower room takes up the remaining space, with a door on either side – it is shared between two compartments. 'Shower room' sounds a bit too glamorous, as it is really just a sink and a shower nozzle and nothing to get very excited about. Other than the smell, the carriage has a rather beaten-up old school grandeur about it. The seats are covered in patterned red silk covers, and the trimmings were once polished hardwood.

The corridor has an ornate patterned blue carpet, and at one end of the carriage there are two rooms, one for the on duty guard, which is a small combined kitchen and communications centre, the other a sleeping room. At this end there is also a locked bathroom, for Chinese use only apparently. Down at the other end of the carriage is the passenger toilet. Scary but functional, it is a Western toilet which simply flushes onto the tracks, and next to it there is a metal sink which on a good day produces a trickle of warm water. Rather worryingly, behind the toilet is a set of huge wooden tongs. I just can't imagine a plumbing scenario in which they might be needed, and these will continue to haunt me in my future train-based nightmares. The trick with the toilet is to be prepared for the steam. That's right, steam! The toilet would just freeze solid were it not for the ingenious system of using hot water from the coal-fired samovar to flush it. Thus, as you deposit the contents of the pan into the Siberian wilderness below with a press of the foot pedal, the hot water meets the outside temperature and whooshes back inside as a rapidly rising cloud of condensing liquid. I learn to stand well back after trying this for the first time.

Beyond the toilet are the inner carriage doors. These lead to a small space at the end of the coach where bags of coal, vegetables and cardboard boxes of anything official are unofficially stored. There is no heating out there, so only things that can be frozen survive very long. Here, too, are the outside doors, on both sides of the train, and going forwards is a door that leads through to the next carriage. The handles of this door are frozen and a small window is frosted over. Beyond it might just be the vacuum of space.

The setup is the same at the other end of the carriage, too. The only difference is a game-changing bit of kit opposite the toilet. Here stands our samovar, the vast and complicated water boiler that can be used to make tea as well as heat water for the plumbing. Nothing is hidden from view – it is a mass of small industrial looking pipes, valves and gauges. Mr Chen takes pity on me the first time I try to use it, showing me temperature gauge and how to turn the vital handle without scalding myself. I make a mental note of its operating procedure and hope there will be no accidental boiler explosions on this trip.

With some time on my hands, back in my compartment I unpack the rest of my bags and squeeze them back under the seats. The place is beginning to resemble home; I love journeys that allow the luxury of being able to unpack. On my table I have a pressed white Chinese Railways tablecloth, my trusty *Flying Scotsman* thermos flask, a bottle of Stolichnaya vodka (I don't drink vodka, but it seems like the done thing) and some guidebooks. Chinese Railways have thoughtfully also provided a vase containing some plastic flowers and a metal tray with some tea-making accessories. Once I've got bored of playing around with the layout of all my stuff in this small space, I decide it's time to explore beyond the door at the rear end of Carriage no 9, to find the mythical restaurant car.

I pass Mr Li, crouched down in the outer corridor. He is frying up some freshly made dumplings in a mini-wok over the open fire. They smell good, but sadly this food is only for the guards. Checking with him that I am headed in the right direction, I prise open the outer door and head into the icy world between the carriages for the first time. There is a definite technique to acquire here. My short arms don't reach the handle on the next carriage door, so I have to shut the first door, let go and pirouette freestyle over the metal floor plates across no man's land, hoping to grab one of the handrails on the far side. This works first time, apart from my hand sticking to the frozen metal: clearly, I need to wear gloves when doing this. I repeat the process as I make my way backwards through four carriages before reaching the restaurant. Twenty-five doors have to be opened and closed. My hands hurt from the cold and get covered in soot. Without gloves this is a Catch 22 situation, as in the restaurant car there is no toilet to wash your hands in. But if you were to wash your hands in the carriage before the restaurant, you would never get there because they would completely stick to the handles as their moisture froze onto the icy metal.

I had read that the restaurant car is a big deal on the Trans-Siberian, and now I was on it myself I was beginning to see why. It's the social centre of the train, and a place to escape the imprisonment of your compartment. This may be because you're lonely if you are by yourself, or desperate to escape your cabin mates if sharing with up to three random strangers. Amongst its attractions other than food are an almost infinite amount of space, black market alcohol, gambling, currency dealing and dodgy movies. Whatever you need you can probably find it here. But top of my list on this morning is food.

The train always has a 'native' restaurant car, from the country you are travelling in. This will therefore be the first of no less than three different restaurants on this leg of my journey. I've had visions of opening the final door, here in Siberia, to reveal a packed carriage of mad Russians drinking vodka and singing patriotic songs. In fact the truth is that there are not many takers for breakfast this morning. To start with there is just me. In front of me are wooden booth-type seats with green plastic cushions up and down both sides of the carriage. There is a bar at one end, and beyond that is a kitchen. As I sit down, a man appears as if by magic. He is middle-aged and a bit scruffy, and looks like he has had less sleep than me. I chance it that the international word for breakfast might be breakfast, and ask for 'breakfast'. I'm disappointed with the outcome as he just walks off, but then he returns a couple of minutes later with a big red plastic book. This is the menu, and I'm rather relieved to find that it contains an English translation. There are lots of dishes, some that I even recognise, but I have been warned that many might not actually be available. I strike lucky first time, though, and successfully order ham and eggs with bread and coffee. The man relays the orders to a kind-looking lady in the kitchen, who I am guessing is his wife. As I discover later, when not cooking they watch soap operas on a laptop or play weird Russian techno music. They have a small dog, and they live in the restaurant car at night. This might yet turn out to be a Siberian remake of *Fawlty Towers*.

A man arrives and sits down in the booth opposite me. He can't be a Russian, as he's wearing a beany hat and smiling. Stefan comes from Hamburg and is also headed to Beijing. We compare notes and plans over breakfast. He lives in Carriage no 10 which, like me, he currently has all to himself. He thinks that there is an Italian woman in one of the other carriages, too, but there is no sign of her in the restaurant yet.

My breakfast is surprisingly edible, apart from the stale bread. Settling the bill (330 rubles; £6), I arrange to see Stephan for a beer at 07:00, but we forget to agree what time zone this appointment is based upon. It will be sometime between 05:00 and 08:00, and as I have nothing else in my diary; I will be there early and also late.

When I get back to my carriage I find that Mr Li and Mr Chen are once again supervising the train engineer unblocking our drains. The go-to solution is to pour a huge metal kettleful of boiling water down the pipe and then probe it with a long bit of wire. I leave them to it, and fetch some water to make some proper coffee. Back in my compartment I get the map out. I have marked my route on it and noted the main stops and their approximate distance from Edinburgh. We have already covered 1,194 km, despite the rather slow speed of the train. The reason for this is that we are nearly always moving, stopping only perhaps four to six times every day.

Out the window I'm looking for the Ural mountain range to orientate myself with the map. I seem to have got completely used to the movement of the train. The only problem occurs when the brakes freeze and there is some kinetic effect of slowing, throwing the carriages around a bit. I have a name for this manoeuvre; it's a Crazy Ivan. They can be quite severe – strong enough to throw you out of bed if you're not wedged in. Right now, though, it's just a rhythmic rattle, and the movement is smooth.

I manage to mentally screen out the commotion in the corridor. The blockage of the drain is now occupying several more members of the Chinese crew – there are buckets of hot water, and assorted spanners and mops next door. We have started to flood. I am beginning to realise that having the supposed luxury of the en-suite dripping tap can be a liability in Siberia. I hope they manage to fix it before the stinking puddle reaches my compartment. As if this isn't enough to contend with, the temperature in the carriage has been steadily rising, to combat the falling temperature outside. The pipes under the train might be frozen, but it's getting really hot in here. Mr Chen is nearly always busy stoking our fire. You can hear him shovel more coal off the frozen metal of the outer carriage floor every couple of hours. Of course he knows better than I do what temperatures we might face tonight.

Before I left home, a few of my friends had questioned what I might get up to whilst imprisoned in my carriage on the longest train journey in the world. Being honest, I wasn't quite sure myself. But what I have now discovered is that a self-absorbing routine quickly emerges, one in which I feel that I actually have no spare time. Station stops and meals provide regular pauses during the day, bracketing my reading, writing, eating and sleeping. After a quick afternoon nap (maybe my sleep wasn't so good last night?) I dress for dinner. I choose a pair of shorts, a t-shirt, gloves and plastic sandals. The finishing touch is a torch that I wear on my head. It's getting too hot for anything else, and I doubt the staff in the restaurant will really care that I have left my dinner suit at home. It's a weird look, and I make sure that there is no photographic evidence of it.

As I arrive back in the restaurant car, the dog hides under a table while Mr Chef and Mrs Chef watch what looks to be a rather violent Russian soap opera. Stefan is already here; he's obviously running on local time. The beer is cold and plentiful. We conclude that there are actually lots of Russians at the back of the train, but as they don't get off at stops unless they have to (for vodka) and don't dine in the restaurant (far too expensive) the train feels deserted. While I'm nurturing my third can of Baltika #7 we discuss various things, some mundane travel chat – and then the bombshell. He tells me that he is a fan of polygamy, and is seeking people to add to his like-minded group in Hamburg. Would I be interested? I listen to a friendly sales pitch on the joys of being a non-possessive lover, but perhaps realising that I'm a repressed British ex-public schoolboy, he soon gives up. We discuss something easier, like the rising carriage temperature and the price of Russian railway beer.

A few other local passengers drift in for dinner during the evening. They drink vodka and eat things like gherkins and potatoes. I get the impression that Russians use the train for overnight journeys between interim cities, rather than all the way from Moscow to Peking. I try to imagine what they do for a living. Some are obviously soldiers; others might be travelling salesmen or arms dealers for all I know. After about 21:00 the violent and also quite adult soap on the laptop is switched off, and Mr Chef chooses some techno music to play on his sound system. I decide that it's time to pay the bill and head for bed.

Arriving back in Carriage no 9, I find that Mr Li has turned in for the night, and Mr Chen is stoking up our fire once again. I'm pleased to see that the flood has gone, and I celebrate this by pouring myself a glass of Spanish wine. I carefully choose the moment to pour, as the train rocks and grinds its way towards our next stop at a place called Tumen. With the door locked and the lights dimmed, my compartment has a nice feel to it. My nostrils have thankfully normalised the smell, and it feels quite cosy inside this small space. If only I could open the window to allow some fresh air in – but it appears to be locked shut. I sit back in my berth and reflect on a good induction day. I'm now a seasoned Trans-Siberian traveller.

Day Ten, Ishim, Russian Federation

Distance travelled so far: 5,962 km

Moscow time (GMT+3)

Station	Arrival	Stop	Departure
Tumen	03:54	20	04:14
Ishim	07:52	12	08:04
Omsk	11:24	16	11:40
Balabinsk	15:26	23	15:49
Novosibirsk	19:13	19	19:32
Taiga	22:35	02	22:37

The first thing that I hear the next morning is one of the guards rolling up the thick insulated blinds that cover the windows in our corridor at night. I am learning the meaning of new sounds each day. Snow and ice have changed my perception of both light and noise. The brightness of the snow tricks you into thinking it might be a warm sunny day, but it could be a whiteout with freezing fog.

Sounds are intensified as they bounce and echo off the snow and ice. At times during last night I heard Russian women chanting station announcements over the platform address system, crunching steps as people walked past my window in the snow, and violent banging as engineers attack the ice forming around the wheels and underside of the train with metal poles. When we're on the move, I find that the rhythm of the train in motion is actually quite soporific and I have managed to get some quite good sleep.

Outside my door in the corridor there is a single sheet of laminated A4 paper, housed in a wooden frame on the wall. To my knowledge it is the only bit of paper on the train that appears in Chinese and Russian and English. It is our timetable. This is a document of almost religious importance to the Trans-Mongolian adventurer. Everything revolves around it, and to decode its secrets gives one great powers. It can be read in both directions, so the first step is to learn to read the correct column either up or down, depending on if you are headed east or west. It rather reminds me of a dive table, the sort scuba enthusiasts use to work out how long they can spend under water. For each stop you can see the time (just to keep you on your toes, it's Moscow time in Russia, but local time in Mongolia and China). Next to this is the length of time of the stop, and then the time the train is due to depart. On my first day I had been relying on Mr Li to tell me how long I had, but with this now decrypted, I can better plan the day ahead. There is no longer any need for international sign language on matters of routine timetable questions.

I had read about the consequences of Moscow time before setting off. One single time zone for train timetables sounds very sensible if you are sat in Moscow office scheduling thousands of trains each day. But out here in Siberia, there's a snag. Each day as we're heading east, we cross into a new local time zone. The train might stop in Moscow time, but the locals live in local time and our restaurant car uses a bit of both. Each day we are straddled a further hour away from Moscow, and this gap is growing. Breakfast in Moscow is already lunch locally, and will become dinner later in the week. I decide to take immediate action and put my watch forward two hours, creating my own approximate local time zone. This makes the Moscow timetable almost incomprehensible without some cross-checking and arithmetic. I realise the solution would be to have one of those watches with more than one time zone, or even a second watch which keeps Moscow time.

At just before 08:00 (Moscow time) we pull into place called Ishim, population 65,243, GMT+5. Up and down the train, the guards are all out in their overcoats, armed with big metal poles. At one end of the platform there is the now familiar sight of the tractor with trailer laden with fresh coal. I decide to stay on board and carry out my ablutions. This feels like a good plan until I find that the toilets are locked – this is standard Trans-Siberian procedure, 10 minutes or so before arriving at a station. I am in a bit of a dilemma about the toilet thing. As a single man with sole use of a private compartment, I have brought along a pee bottle that I can use at night. If that sounds a bit specialist, it's actually a sports water bottle, but I had carefully marked it to avoid any unfortunate errors. I was planning to simply empty this down my en-suite sink that I wasn't sharing with anyone else at this stage. But I have changed my mind. Given that the sink drain is prone to freezing up overnight, my plan could all go horribly wrong, and for several days I would have to suffer the consequences of living in a frozen urinal.

Pondering on this and a few other environ-mental problems – mainly that it's getting really hot in my carriage – I postpone my ablutions and head to the restaurant car for some breakfast. It's a bit busier today, and I spot someone having sausage and scrambled eggs, a dish definitely not on the menu. Is there a secret menu with special orders that I don't know about? I take a photo of it before anyone can deny it had ever existed, and show it to a woman I have not seen before, who is taking the orders. I rather hope that as a newly established regular I will also be granted the privilege of ordering things not on the menu. She takes my phone away to show the picture to Mr Chef – surely she must know how to say 'scrambled eggs' to Mr Chef in Russian? Anyway, the deal is done. I'm now in the secret breakfast club.

After a passable meal I order a second cup of the thick muddy-tasting black coffee and ignore the dog as it scampers underneath my table in search of the possibility of a misplaced sausage. I smile to myself as I manage to recite pretty accurately part of the script from the *Fawlty Towers* episode 'The Kipper and the Corpse'. I get about as far as 'Don't you have dogs in Calcutta?' before realising the train is slowing down again. I need to plan around the stops better, as all my cold weather gear is in my own carriage, which is of course twenty-five doors away. No time to hang around. The handwritten bill makes no sense to me, but Mrs Chef shows me the price on her large Casio calculator. With that settled I leave Little Russia for the day.

We stop at Omsk bang on schedule at 11:24 for 20 minutes. In what I'm already used to as standard procedure, we take on more coal for the fires, and the locomotive is changed for a new one (these are electric, with overhead power lines as far as the Mongolian border). Just in case you are a trainspotter, I can confirm our locomotive today is now a ChS2. This I know as there is a picture of it in my Trans-Siberian handbook.

Mr Li has one polished English phrase, which is 'ten minutes!' – he says this to me each time I get off, so far usually stopping for up to 20 minutes. I'm not complaining, though, as he has my interests at heart and keeps an eye on me when I'm on the platform. Last night I heard tales of guards in other carriages who were not at all helpful, so I have been lucky to have him in Carriage no 9. Feeling a bit more relaxed and less fearful of getting left behind, I stroll along the platform to Carriage no 8, which would seem to be where most of the train officials are living.

I have noticed that we have a sort of Chinese commander-in-chief-in-chief and a second-in-command or sergeant major. They are only really noticeable when we stop and from what I can see must spend the rest of their time in their compartments playing cards. The commander-in-chief is in his twenties and wears a long military-style blue coat and an officer's *ushanka*. He strolls along the platform supervising the loading of coal and goods. His much older and rail-savvy number two walks with him everywhere, and wears a tank commander-in-chief's type of leather jacket and an *ushanka* with the earflaps sticking out at a jaunty angle. They make quite an impressive-looking double act. Whilst they supervise, all the other guards are busy loading coal, and they also load the post into a carriage right behind the locomotive. When it is time to get going, the commander-in-chief gives the signal to saddle up, and just like in *Von Ryan's Express* the guards get back onto the train. Any travellers still on the platform at this point get a vaguely threatening final wave from the sergeant major. If you have never seen *Von Ryan's Express*, it's a ripping yarn of wartime train adventure, but in my opinion Trevor Howard plays the one-dimensional cynical officer character far too often for his own good.

The platform is the best place to meet Russians, as they don't visit the restaurant or move about in the Chinese section of the train very much. Outside, they buy their food and chain-smoke. Those I have met so far have been pretty friendly, offering me a local cigarette and just about smiling as we stand there in the snow and ice. They try out their English, which is a million times better than my Russian, and I seem to make a few friends. Rather bizarrely, some of them don't bother to dress up for the platform and stand there in shorts, like this is normal behaviour for the truly hardy Russian man. Many of the soldiers don't bother to put their boots on, and the conscripts look weird in full combat gear and flip-flops in the snow.

As we make our way east, I am noticing more people. The problem is that everyone appears to be on different time zones and movement patterns. Some are in hibernation; others appear just for cigarettes at food resupply in the big stations. I have now counted twelve non-Russian travellers. In the evening they drift in and out of the restaurant car, where they read or chat. Most are in *kupe* class – sharing four-berth compartments. There is a slightly scary and very independent Italian woman, two lovely Swedish ladies, a fearless family of four Australians, and three German men, who seem to be serious adventurers. We are all headed to Beijing except the Australians, who get off in Ulan Bator. I get the impression things will change as we approach Mongolia: Ulan Bator is a popular jumping on point for travellers, and also where the cross-border traders load up the train with all sorts of goods.

I discover over lunch (pickled herrings, bread) that the restaurant car operates a black market as well as an above-the-counter operation. Each of the seats have smuggler's compartments underneath them, and these are full of vodka, beer and goodies. I guess it's a nice little side-line for the Russians who run the restaurant, and a bit mad that prices of over-the-counter food and drink is so high for the average local. Considering the success of the way Russia has transformed itself from extreme communism to extreme capitalism, I return to my base. As I cover the twenty-five doors, I bump into the resident engineer in Carriage no 7. He has all sorts of plumbing jobs under way in other carriages. Trans-Mongolian plumbing looks like a full-time occupation. One of the second class carriages I walk through is a particularly grim sight. It's very cold, and there is a big water escape at one end, and everyone looks miserable.

I have developed an updated procedure for moving between the carriages. The Russian carriages have a light outside in no man's land, but the Chinese carriages (most of the train) don't, so the head torch being on first really helps. It's a scary place to be in the dark, alone and shut out of both carriages in the freezing atmosphere of the outside world. What I do now is to shut the first door behind me but, still holding the door handle, I put one foot over to the next carriage and grasp the second door handle, ignoring the icy railings. Then I leap across. I also pack wet wipes and a small travel towel in my day bag. This allows me to clean any soot off in the restaurant without my hands sticking to anything. Chinese trains provide bedding but not towels, so I'm making do with one of those super-absorbent camping towels. It's a glorified flannel, really, but does the job.

During the afternoon we slowly cross the Baraba steppe, the train stops at Barabinsk (population 30,394) at 15:26 for 22 minutes. My guidebook doesn't have much to say about the place, so I just spend 5 minutes sucking in freezing air on the platform. There is a bit of retail therapy here. At bigger stops there seem to be three options: people standing on the platform selling things; kiosks on the platform selling things; and most risky – proper shops outside the station. I'm just not brave enough yet to try the last option. Here in Barabinsk, fur-coated women outside on the platform are selling dried fish, coffee beans and plastic bottles of what I guess is local moonshine. I decide to pass on these fine dining options today, and I just buy some water from a kiosk. I have been decanting hot water from the samovar into a metal water bottle and drinking it once it is cold, but it doesn't taste very nice.

Back on board I have to face up to an emerging problem. I need to do something about the temperature in my compartment. I don't have a thermometer (wish I had packed one) but it must be over 30°C. I wish I could open the window, but it has no obvious parts to unlock.

It's time to speak to Mr Li. I send a climate delegation of just myself, representing 100 per cent of the passengers in the carriage, to his day compartment. He is sat there, methodically peeling vegetables and drinking tea. Outside his compartment in my shorts and t-shirt, I make the best international signs that I can for 'Don't you think it's getting a bit too hot in here?' I must have watched too much of the television game show *Give Us a Clue* as a child – Mr Li seems to immediately get my hot mime. Lionel Blair would have approved. What happens next sums up Chinese ingenuity: Li picks up a folded blanket and sets off down the corridor towards the toilet. I follow, not quite sure if I am to have a further role in the procedure. He then wedges open the toilet door with the tongs I'd seen on my first visit to the toilet, pushes up a ceiling tile and wedges the blanket in, leaving the roof void open. Blissful cool air immediately flows down the corridor. It's a good result, as long as I'm okay about using the toilet with the door open.

I had one other idea to try out, as the cooler air in the corridor isn't going to help my compartment at night if my door is closed. So, inspired by NASA, I improvise a heat shield – a roll of several sheets of tin foil gaffer-taped over the radiator in my compartment, to hopefully hold back some of the heat. It's a clever idea, but it seems to make no significant difference. I shall think about its design some more tomorrow. If only I can find a valve in the hot water pipe, I could turn it down, but the designer hasn't considered that passengers might want to have their own choice of temperature. Clearly it's a centrally planned Chinese asset.

In the early evening we make a stop at Novosibirsk. If Siberian station platforms look bleak during the day, then you should see them at night. A frozen world partly illuminated by big gantries of strong sodium lights. A place where people dare not stop moving, and chain-smoke to stay warm. Mrs Chef hurries across the tracks and leaves the station to get fresh provisions. I hope she makes it back in time (22 minutes, or when we have loaded enough coal) as I'm looking forward to a spot of supper later on. Other than the obvious hazard of getting run over, another problem I can see for her is that if a train arrives on a platform between the shop and the platform she might well be stuck. I guess she might be able to climb through the doors of a passenger train, but many of them are freight – almost endless trains of oil, lumber and ore crossing the continent. From ground level these trains look really huge, and you have a sense of how fragile humans are, moving about around them. The ground shakes when they move past, and close up the rumble is deafening.

With nothing else in my diary I decide to supervise the changing of the engine. I make my way up front, where the driver has already uncoupled his massive red locomotive. He waves at me, toots the horn and heads off, leaving me alone. I don't think I can remember being more isolated than standing there at this moment. I don't last long enough to see the arrival of the new engine, as it's just too cold. Even my trusty camera refuses to switch on. The solution is to keep it inside my down jacket until the last possible moment and swap batteries after every stop, so it's fully charged and has a warm battery.

Back in the restaurant car, I drink beer until the restaurant closes, 20:00 Moscow time, 01:00 local time. Our supply of Baltika No. 7 has now run out, so have switched to Baltika No. 3. It is no longer necessary to put them in the fridge; just give the cans 20 minutes in the outer corridor and they're almost too cold. Mrs Chef manages to rustle up a pork escalope and some burned fried potato slices served with a tastefully arranged garnish of indeterminate items of salad. The food is fine if you are not too fussy, but it is expensive and I can understand why many of the Russians choose to dine on instant noodles in their compartments.

As I wander back through the carriages I get a slice of the life of other passengers. The flood in Carriage no. 7 now appears to be under control. I think the toilets are still closed and the samovar is out of order, but the manly men with screwdrivers are still hard at work fixing them. It remains very cold in there. Carriage no. 8 is like the *Mary Celeste*. The clue is the number of power extension leads daisy-chained into the single socket in the corridor and routed under the carpet into the compartments. Here I suspect the off-shift guards, the commander-in-chief-in-chief and his adjutant are bingeing on Russian soap operas. Back in Carriage no 9, I can see sparks flying past the window again – Mr Li has been busy with his coal shovelling – are we on fire again? It's certainly hot enough to imagine we might be.

Back at my compartment, I find that my door has been locked by one of the guards. It doesn't feel unsafe, but people do sometimes pass through from other carriages, so I trust the guards' judgement. I feel a bit smug and for the first time I use my British Gas meter cupboard key to undo the lock. I wish I had thought this through. When Mr Li sees me sat inside, I'm the subject of a crime scene investigation. How did I get in? I have to shrug a lot and use the language barrier to cover my tracks. I point down the corridor as though another guard has opened my door. As a result of this alibi, Li wanders off looking puzzled. I think Li and Chen have been comparing notes, and my story doesn't add up; neither of them can work out how I managed to unlock my compartment without their help. I even wonder if I might be hauled in front of the train commander-in-chief for further questioning, but this doesn't happen. They eye me suspiciously, but nothing more is said.

The local time zone is beginning to be a problem. This afternoon it got dark at about 14:45 Moscow time. I have decided to start moving my watch further towards Mongolian time (+4 hours, GMT+8) but of course I still need to know both Moscow time (on which the train timetable runs) and my own time zone (on which local life and the kitchen run). I hope it will work, but it means an earlier start tomorrow to make the most of the short day – I've set my watch two hours forward before turning in, and will do the same tomorrow. That means when I get to the Mongolian border on Saturday I will be in the correct time zone and avoid a big jump.

Eight: Ice Cold in Irkutsk

Day Eleven, Ilanskaya, Russian Federation
Distance travelled so far: 7,622 km

Moscow time (GMT+3)

Station	Arrival	Stop	Departure
Minsk	00:34	25	00:59
Krasnoyarsk	06:30	20	06:50
Ilanskaya	10:52	20	11:12
Nizhne-Udinsk	15:42	12	15:54
Zima	19:17	3	19:47
Irkutsk	23:25	25	23:50

My perception of what 'cold' means is slowly changing. When I first arrived in Russia, the temperatures were remarkable only for being different from what I was used to. (British people tend to panic easily about minus figures, and can describe a few days of -5°C as a weather bomb. Public transport tends to fall apart quickly in cold weather, and I think this is mainly because the temperature fluctuates across the freezing point too often – this is much harder to manage than a constantly frozen environment.) So until now, temperature has been just a rather exotic negative number. Other than my camera not working and my hands sticking to bare metal, life goes on.

But here in Ilanskaya this morning the coldness is far more debilitating. There is actually a lot less snow about now – but it's brutally cold. I got off the train to have a look at the new locomotive being hooked up whilst we took on more coal. The temperature has dropped further since yesterday. There was no thermometer on the platform (often there is a digital clock and thermometer displayed above the station hall) but a railway worker laughed about the climate (or was he laughing at me?) and wrote '-35' in dust on the side of the train. It is a bright and sunny day, but the air is painful to breathe and my trousers no longer protect my legs enough for me to last more than a few minutes outside. Getting back into the heat of the carriage is now a painful experience, as my circulation slowly returns to my limbs.

I was lucky enough to once meet Sir Ran Fiennes at the Royal Geographical Society in London. I shall never forget that meeting. After the lecture he spoke to me in such a slow and gentle way, studying me in great detail, as if to assess my chances of becoming a successful adventurer. His eyes were gentle and probing. When we shook hands and I said farewell, I felt as if I had been blessed. In explorer terms it was like meeting the Pope or the Dalai Lama. I'm not a religious person, but from that moment on I felt I had extra resolve and commitment. Whenever I feel a bit low or have a problem, my challenge to myself now is, 'What would Ran do?' Back then I hoped that I would learn to cope with the cold, but I knew that if I got frostbite I would draw the line at his solution of hacksawing the ends of my fingers off.

Stephan (the chap from Hamburg, in the next first class carriage) went to see our train commander-in-chief on the platform at Ilanskaya to ask if he could move into a warmer carriage, like mine. If only he better understood the problems that I was having because of the heat. I tried to explain, but 'warmer' just sounded good to him. For some reason his carriage is kept at what I think is a much more reasonable temperature, maybe 20°C. Carriage no 9 by comparison is more jungle-like, at well over 30°C. I join him to give some moral support, and we rather shyly approach the gaggle of heavy-overcoated senior Chinese officials. The conversation takes place in broken English, but is translated by the RSM into Mandarin for the benefit of the commander-in-chief.

Sadly Stephan's case is a foregone conclusion. I

now understand that there is no single word for 'no' in Mandarin. So after what sounds like a few sentences full of possibilities in Chinese, the sergeant major translates this for us as just 'No'. Our C-in-C smiles, but the look he gives suggests that if he spoke English he would be saying, 'Don't be a foolish foreigner. You should be thankful that you have a cabin. What will you want next? Breakfast in bed?'

So my carriage gets to remain empty, apart from myself, Mr Li and Mr Chen. As our negotiation is taking place on the platform, Russian fighter jets screech past. They fly over the train several times, afterburners engaged in full reheat. Are they practising bombing runs on the train or practising protecting us? This is a world away from Clapham Junction. I think they are MiG-35s, but I don't ask anyone to confirm this for me. I decide not take a photograph, just in case I am branded a spy and removed from the train. But I know the amazing fact that in the Russian Federation today, if you have hard currency and a satisfactory medical you can buy a seat in a plane like this and fly to the edge of space for about £18,000. I'm not sure what the founders of MiG, Mr Mikoyan and Mr Gurevich, would think about that.

Sat in my sauna – sorry, compartment – I write my diary and update my blog. I'm dressed in just a pair of shorts and a tee shirt to cope with the tropical climate of Carriage no 9. I have got into a sort of routine of downloading pictures from my camera after every stop, and recharging the camera whilst I write. My writing stimulation is provided by strong, freshly home-brewed coffee and the amazingly brightly lit snowscape outside. On my table I have my guidebooks, my watch, my coffee-making kit and the gear to sort my camera out. I often play music on my iPad. Today it's a bit of a Steely Dan back catalogue day. Steely Dan always make me feel upbeat and optimistic, and their discovery was a great gift to me from my older brother. Today I'm listening to 'Can't Buy a Thrill' and 'Countdown to Ecstasy'.

The time zone issue continues to confuse me. I'm no longer sure if my breakfast is my lunch, or my lunch is in fact my dinner. This will all sort itself out on the Mongolian frontier, so I'll just have to stay straddled in two different time zones for a couple of days more. In my spare time I think with my stomach, and I realise that I'm getting a bit bored with the Russian restaurant car. The food has been better than I was expecting, but the novelty of some of the dishes has now worn off, and my diet is one-dimensional, oily and often overcooked. I wanted to try some pancakes with jam today for my breakfast, but although they are on the menu Mr Chef, unaccountably, doesn't seem keen to make them. The thing that gets to me the most about the catering is that the service is always provided with a sense of overwhelming indifference and unhappiness. Still, in two days we will uncouple the Russian restaurant car and add a Mongolian one. I'm quite excited by the prospect of this, as I hear it can be quite good – especially if you like mutton. In my dreams, though, I fantasise about a roast turkey with all the trimmings. I wonder what might be possible once I reach Beijing, as this is where I shall spend my Christmas Day.

A new character has appeared in the restaurant car this evening. His name is Dmitri, and he is a young paramedic from Ulan-Ude. He speaks a few words of English, and Stephan engages him in conversation using his mobile phone as a translator whenever we get stuck. It works remarkably well, and many icy beers are consumed. As the conversation becomes more complex, some charades are needed to decode certain things. We become stuck on the word for a particularly smelly type of dried fish from Lake Baikal. This becomes comedy gold, like the charade in the Spanish torture scene in the Blackadder II episode, 'Chains': 'Oh, it's a scythe!'

Supper is becoming predictable in everything but cost. By far the best dishes on the menu have been the smoked salmon (with stale brown bread), and the pork escalope, served with singed strips of oily potato. I carry a small box of condiments that I have brought from the UK so I can spice things up a bit. The pork takes on a flavour all of its own with an accompaniment of my Tabasco sauce and mustard.

At the far end of the restaurant is a door that I have never been through before. It leads to what we call the Russian Sector. This comprises of the slowly diminishing number of Russian carriages attached to the end of our otherwise Chinese train. I don't see many Russian people, because they are nearly all in there, on the other side of the restaurant. Only the few Russians travelling internationally are in the Chinese carriages further up the train.

Stephan and I decide to do our bit for international relations and pay a state visit tonight. Passing through the door at the unfamiliar end of the restaurant car past the kitchen, we find a door to a strangely different-looking world. The design of the door is unfamiliar, and more modern than the part of the train we know. Once across the gap and into the RZD (Russian) carriage, we get about five paces before meeting the *provodnitsa*. Her name is Rita, and she seems pleased to see us, but concerned about our intentions. All the other Russian carriages have already been cut loose tonight, and it turns out that there is just a single remaining carriage of *kupe* compartments here. On board there are an assortment of soldiers and salesmen living on the train in the same style I'd experienced on the train from Warsaw to Moscow. They watch movies on their laptops, and leave their compartment doors mainly open. It looks very relaxed and friendly. At the far end of the carriage I look out the little frosted window to see nothing but the outside world and the tracks behind us – it is the end of the Trans-Mongolian Express. I think Rita is worried that we might try to open the final door to meet an icy fate behind the train. I'm grateful for her concern, and we head back to the restaurant feeling like we were intruding a bit on this separated Russian community. I wish I had ventured back here earlier in the week as I bet that they had some good parties.

Exploration completed for the day, I say goodnight to Stephan as I pass through his nice-temperature carriage and head back to the jungle of Carriage no 9, still at an unhealthy 30°C. Mr Li opens my door (I give him an innocent look, like I have no key) and I strip down to a pair of pants for the night ahead. I spend the rest of the evening finishing off my new invention – the Mark 2 heat shield. I'm quite proud of it, and my construction has all the elements of that scene from the film *Apollo 13*; the one where Tom Hanks has to build a new CO_2 scrubber from a pile of random objects on board the lunar excursion module. I thought that Ron Howard did an amazing job with this film. I only wish that my heat shield would work as well as Jim Lovell's scrubber. (All you need to make one for yourself at home is ten metres of aluminium foil, some cardboard, a tape measure and some gaffer tape.) It's more effective than the Mark 1 shield, as it is ten sheets thick and covers the whole length of the radiator, but it still seems to have only a limited effect.

It is at this point that, in utter desperation, I have a crack at unbolting the window in order to open it, only to realise that I've unwittingly committed an act of serious sabotage – if the window drops off, this will almost certainly be the end of my journey. Perhaps for a long, long time. I try to imagine the commander-in-chief and his sergeant major discovering that my compartment is without its window and completely freaking out (in a Chinese sort of way). Moving quickly, I reassemble the bolts, washers and grommets and get them screwed back in as best as I can. All looks good, but I seem to have three bolts and nowhere to put them, so I hide these under my table. I hope that the window is over-engineered, and they will not be needed to keep it attached to the train, for the rest of this journey at least. I wipe off the sweat with my travel towel and consider myself lucky.

I like to think of myself as a logical thinker, and I'm proud to say that later that night I come up with a cunning temperature reduction plan – one that reduces the temperature of my compartment by about 5°C. The solution is to remove the fixed plug in the sink of my en-suite bathroom and wedge open the door to my sleeping compartment. The sink drains to the outside of the carriage, and as long as it isn't blocked with ice I can feel the flow of cold air coming up out of it. I also decide to sleep on the lower berth. Although it is closer to the radiator, the air is cooler at the bottom of the carriage, and with the curtains open I can also feel some extra coolness through the window. This solution will be workable as long as the compartment next door is empty. The bathroom is shared, and it won't be possible for me to keep my door open and next door's locked. Let's hope that that Carriage no 9 remains unpopular.

I grab some fitful sleep before we pull into Irkutsk at about 04:00 local time, and although it's one of the biggest cities in Siberia, I just don't feel strong enough to get dressed up to explore further. Instead I put my tracksuit on and poke my head out the carriage door. Unsurprisingly, on the platform it is dark and cold. In fact my breath freezes on my beard. I would like to try that experiment you see weathermen do on a really cold day when you throw a cup of coffee in the air and it freezes instantaneously. I'm sure it would work here. After 5 minutes I've had enough, and back in my berth and thinking of other scientific experiments I could perform, I eventually drift back to sleep, this time having nightmares about being sucked out of my compartment through my missing window and into the frozen void outside.

Day Twelve, Ulan-Ude, Russian Federation

Distance travelled so far: 8,889 km

Moscow time (GMT+3)

Station	Arrival	Stop	Departure
Slyudyanka	02:23	02	02:25
Ulan-Ude	07:27	37	08:04
Dzida	12:08	02	12:10
Naushki	13:08	155	16:43
Dozorne	16:54	03	16:57

When I wake the next morning I'm not sure where I am. I don't mean where in the world I am, but where I am on the train. The view from the bottom bunk is very different, and I have to think about this for a few moments before remembering about my nocturnal activities. As soon as I remember, I am relieved to see that I do in fact still have a window. Thinking about the fun we had in the restaurant car the night before, I also have an unnerving feeling that I may have ordered some sort of especially smelly local dried fish. Dmitri seemed very keen on this fish and was arranging for a supply to be hand-delivered at Irkutsk. I get dressed in my tracksuit and flip-flops – very Russian – and head off for some breakfast to discover how much fish I might have accidentally ordered. In the restaurant there is no sign of Dmitri or Stephan, who are probably both enjoying a good lie-in. Some passengers seem to spend all day in bed, but my routine is based around always being up to see what's going on. In a way I envy Dmitri and Stephan, and wish I had allowed myself a few more hours' rest this morning. The ever-advancing time zone combined with the heat on board is seriously tiring me out.

I sit in my usual spot and drink thick strong train coffee whilst looking out at the scenery. The train has been working its way around Lake Baikal, but I think I might have missed the best views during the hours before dawn. I'm distracted from staring out the window by the need to make a big decision about whether to have sausage or ham with my scrambled eggs. Then just for a moment the trees disappear and I get my first glimpse of the lake. It's an amazing sight, so big that it appears more like a frozen sea. My guidebook says it's the largest freshwater lake in the world, holding 20 per cent of the global supply of fresh water. On the shoreline I can see strange crystal-like frozen waves, and then it's just ice to the horizon. I'm still coming to terms with its size and beauty when the lake vanishes again as we pass into a forest. I get the camera out, but even when the lake briefly reappears between forests it's hard, with the dirty windows and low winter sun, to get a good photograph.

There is something different about the restaurant car this morning. With the lake outside I haven't really looked around inside, where Mr Chef has been busy putting up Christmas decorations. It now feels a little bit Christmassy here. I think about this some more. It feels Christmassy because Christmas Day is just two days away. But as Russians follow the Orthodox calendar, the official restaurant car Christmas is more than a week away; I am not just in my own time zone, but in my own advent calendar too. To mark the arrival of the decorations, Mrs Chef presents me with a tangerine after my breakfast. I have brought some small Christmas gifts with me for people on the train, so I hand these out during the morning. I'm pleased that I bothered with this, as the presents had been on my scrapping list when I had too much gear to carry. As I'm the only passenger handing out Christmas gifts, all my rail-based sins are seemingly forgiven. I'm not sure this would have been enough if they knew about what I've done to my window, though.

At close to midday (local time) we pull into Ulan-Ude, our last significant stop in southern Siberia. Having missed Irkutsk, I'm kitted up ready for the stop, and off as soon as Mr Li gets the door open. It needs some encouragement today as it has frozen shut – but a couple of blows on the steps from a big iron bar and it's done. Outside it is of course cold, but the sky is a deep saturated blue and the sun feels strong, giving an illusion of warmth. It's a busy place and I meet the cross-border traders with their piles of boxes containing oranges, eggs, honey, hooch and anything else they probably have hidden. Opposite our train on Platform 4 is another long-distance train – it's the Rossiya, the Russian train travelling the other way, from Vladivostok to Moscow. It's modern-looking and painted red and grey, complete with uniformed staff who look more like they might be the crew of a new low-cost airline. It's very different from our train, which is painted main battle tank green and is much less corporate in appearance.

On the subject of trains and the military, I saw some pictures in Moscow of how Russian trains were until recently used to transport and launch nuclear weapons. Specially built carriages carried SS-24 missiles, each with a 550-kiloton-yield warhead, until 2008. Reports are that a 'railway based combat rocket system' is now secretly back in operation. Since learning about this, I regard any green carriages without windows with some suspicion. There are a couple on the Vladivostok train, but I'm relieved to see that they are just carrying the mail. Unless of course the mail is just a clever military cover story.

In Trans-Siberian standard operating procedure, the engine is uncoupled and leaves us on the platform whilst we take on coal, post and provisions. A new engine backs down onto the train, and its job will be to pull us up towards the Mongolian border later today. A few more people have joined the train in Irkutsk, and most of them hang around territorially outside their carriages, smoking and stocking up on Russian noodles and supplies from the nearby platform kiosks.

I have never seen anything like these shops anywhere else in the world. You can't go inside them; instead they display all their wares in the window and you do business through a small letterbox, like at a post office. It's a bit like a mini version of an Argos store, but in Russian and there is no catalogue. I have no idea what a lot of the items are, or how to ask for them in Russian, so it's a simple point-and-pay system. Noodles, fizzy drinks, postcards, fur slippers, children's toys and cigarettes – everything you might need for a Trans-Siberian adventure. Today I settle on a Pot Potato – a Russian Pot Noodle, and what turns out to be some sort of Siberian sausage roll, which is encouragingly still warm.

Our stop at Ulan-Ude takes a bit longer than the other stops; the reason seems to be that we are stockpiling extra coal. Mr Chen is filling up extra sacks and stacking them by the door. I'm not sure what this means; is it going to get even hotter inside?

It's not too long before the sergeant major is

shouting and gesturing at us all to get back on the train, and we're off again. I don't know what he's shouting, but I imagine it's not very polite, reminding me that I will be in this frozen place forever unless I obey his order to get back on the train right *now*. The line in front of us splits in two: one continues east towards the Russian Far East and Vladivostok, the other in a more southerly direction towards Mongolia and the Gobi desert. Our next major stop will be its capital city, Ulan Bator or UB. Mongolia, here we come!

Back in my compartment I strip off and decide to work on my own Christmas decorations. Even though I'm short of space I decide that a little detail like this will help keep my spirits up, so I have been carrying a small plastic box full of seasonal things. I put some silver tinsel around the window (quite tasteful) and hang up some illuminated ice crystal stars (less tasteful), and on my table I place a flashing mini Christmas tree (not tasteful at all). Mr Chen pretends not to stare in surprise as he walks past my compartment. Mr Lee is clearly impressed by my efforts, and he wishes me a Happy New Year. I leave my door open and enjoy watching even the hardest Russian men smile when they glance in.

The tinsel makes my window look like a big picture frame. Its subject is the constantly changing panorama outside. Things begin to look a bit different as we wind around huge walled farms and river plains. We are criss-crossing a huge river flood plain and hugging the edges of the surrounding hills on each side. It's good for taking pictures, as for the first time I can photograph the whole train as it curves round on itself when it crosses the river. Or at least I could, if my window wasn't smeared with thick red dust and a film of frozen moisture. Stephan has made these photographs into an art form. He uses the ice on his window like a special filter for his lens. He only has a cheap compact camera, but is taking some great pictures.

In the distance there are mountains ahead. The snow on the ground is getting thinner and more powdery as we gradually climb out of the valley and above the treeline. This landscape looks alien after several days of unending *taiga* (forest) and thick snow. Just when I think there is no life whatsoever out there, I spot a beaten-up Lada speeding along a dirt road parallel with the train. The car has a dog in the passenger seat, which stares back at me. Much smoke pours out the car's exhaust of the as it manages to gradually pull ahead of the train. I wonder where they are going in such a hurry.

I pay my final twenty-five-door visit to the restaurant to say goodbye to Mr Chef, Mrs Chef and their helper. I'm still not exactly sure of their relationship, but they seem to get on very well together. The helping lady has been dressing up more each day during the journey, and today she looks like a passable Bond girl villain from the Roger Moore era. The creepy dog also seems pleased to see me. I'm not sure why, as I haven't dropped a sausage all week. They will be uncoupled along with the remaining Russian at the border, and I assume get attached to a train heading back west in a few hours. Although I'm bored with the food, I feel a little sad and strangely emotional about leaving the Russian Sector behind. Perhaps it is because it signals the end of the Siberian part of my adventure, and Siberia is a place I have really enjoyed being in. It has been fascinating to see how Russia has tamed such an inhospitable place and made it possible to live in. Train travel unifies and connects this vast space.

Aware that we will be without a restaurant car tonight, I take an early meal. I eat *solyanka*, a sort of Russian sweet and sour stew, and a final Baltika beer. Most of the Western travellers are here, probably feeling, like me, that they need to pay their last respects to the restaurant. A few people emerge that I have not met before. I can only assume they have been self-catering and sleeping a lot, or perhaps living on Moscow time.

As the sun is about to set we pull in to Naushki, where the Russian border formalities will take place. The sunset is purple and the smoke from the samovar in each carriage rises up into the clear sky. This is my first train border since entering

Belarus, and I'm not sure how things will work. Mr Li and Mr Chen seem pretty relaxed, and we are allowed to get off and wander on the deserted platform. At one end there is a waiting room, and at the other a pile of snow several feet high and big sign pronouncing certain trouble to anyone passing beyond it without permission.

Stephan appears, and he has news: he has been on a recce of the station and found that it has a shower room. At first I find this hard to believe, but he says he is off to get a towel and his things. A few minutes later I tag along and follow him into a small building. Inside there is a lady behind a desk who doesn't seem surprised to see us. She confirms there is a shower here. At first I put it down to something lost in translation, and insist on a guided tour. My wish is granted, and we inspect a single spotless shower, with warm water and towels provided, in a private bathroom, on a platform in the middle of absolutely nowhere.

Stephan is getting on rather well with a nice Turkish-American lady called Ceyda, who joined us at last night in Irkutsk. I wonder if he has told her about the polygamy thing yet. Personal hygiene being a factor in his success, he calls shotgun and dives in first after paying the custodian a few rubles. I go and fetch my wash bag and stand in the adjoining waiting room like an expectant father waiting for news of what's going on next door. The waiting room is a sterile place, with no information, people or activity what-soever.

Thinking about my shower, I begin to get panicky. My worst train-based nightmare, about being left behind, grows bigger in my mind with each minute that passes. I visualise the train moving off towards the border and me chasing after it down the icy platform in just my towel and slippers. I would have to survive with just the contents of my wash bag. I decide that I'm not going to take the risk. Resigned to my continued slightly grubby state, I trudge back to Carriage no 9. The platform is eerily quiet – no activity, no engine, no kiosks. Just nine solitary Chinese carriages and the smell of burning coal.

Mr Li lowers the steps and lets me back on board. Once I am in my compartment, he hands me a small pile of papers and indicates that I should complete them without delay. Nothing like a bit of paperwork at a border, so I dig out my travel documents and start to fill in each of them in carefully in black ink. Some countries seem to have figured out how to design forms much better than others, and I smile at a few of the seemingly irrelevant questions. I take great pride in the correct completion of red tape. I always imagine that such documents will be graded, and I strive to be top of the class – I am aiming for a gold star and an immigration pat on the back, but of course it never comes.

Nothing happens for half an hour, so I decide to start preparing dinner. I'm self-catering tonight, and the menu is Pot Potato, crackers, pâté and cheese, with chocolate biscuits for desert. One of my Trans-Siberian catering innovations has been the creation of a minibar; because you can chill down almost anything in hour or so in the outer part of the carriage, I have converted an old cardboard box into a place to stash beer and wine. The idea is that it blends in with all the other boxes and doesn't get stolen. I prepare the minibar for later this evening and hide it next to the newly filled sacks of frozen coal. Just as I'm doing this I can hear the slamming of doors up and down the train, and a whole load of officials arrive. These include Russian police, army, sniffer dogs, immigration, and plain clothes people with torches – it's a busy place all of a sudden. I hope that Stephan has finished his shower and made it back okay.

My Christmas decorations are working a treat, and apart from the sniffer dogs all the officials seem to appreciate my efforts – even some of the severest-looking security officers allow themselves a smile when they see my mini Christmas tree flashing away. I doubt that it is the behaviour of a smuggler to decorate one's compartment in this way, and I hope it might help break the ice a bit. That, or get me taken away for further questioning.

My passport and forms are checked and then taken away by a man with a briefcase. A customs officer comes in to see me and takes a good look round. She asks me if I have anything to declare, so I show her my wine stash. She looks at me as if to say that I might not actually have enough booze, before wishing me a Happy Christmas and heading off to find some real smugglers. An immigration lady returns my stamped passport, and I think it's all over, but in another few minutes there is another woman searching my compartment. She asks me to step out into the corridor. I can see that she takes pride in being thorough as she turns the place over, inspecting random items of my luggage.

One good aspect of border crossings by train is that officials mostly come to visit you rather than the other way around. I realise that the trick is to just relax and go about my business of being a train adventurer whilst looking respectful (and respectable) to each official as they visit me. I pour myself a glass of reasonable Spanish wine and sit back until the next official arrives. When the next person arrives, I stand up and greet them, trying to show as much respect as possible. Most ask me to take my glasses off and stare at me for quite a long time before deciding that I am actually the same person as the dashing chap pictured in my passport.

Dinner is a relaxed but lonely affair, and I

spread out the courses between the immigration and customs interviews. My movie selection is *Spies Like Us* (1985) – Dan Aykroyd and Chevy Chase at their very best, set amidst a Cold War world that I feel must have been very similar to what is going on just outside my door right now. The evening passes slowly, but we are still on schedule. Over the course of an hour I see about a dozen people in all, each wanting to see my passport, my paperwork or my belongings. All this is just to facilitate leaving Russia, so I wonder what entering Mongolia might entail. I shall soon find out.

Nine: Thirsty Camel

Day Thirteen, Suhe-Bator, Mongolia
Distance travelled so far: 9,142 km

Ulan Bator time (GMT+8)

Station	Arrival	Stop	Departure
Suhe-Bator	21:30	105	23:15
Darhan	00:48	17	01:05
Zonhala	03:15	25	03:40
Ulan Bator	06:30	45	07:15
Choyr	11:33	20	11:53
Sain-Shanda	15:06	37	15:43
Dzamynude	19:10	85	20:35

I am finally admitted to Mongolia late at night, and we trundle out of the border station of Suhe-Bator after midnight, a little behind schedule. Towards the end of the evening the border formalities had become a bit farcical. After two more searches of my compartment, one involving a lady with an electric screwdriver, I was given the classic good cop/bad cop ruse. A friendly man stepped into my carriage, shook me by the hand and wished me a nice trip to Mongolia. At first I thought he might be a black market currency trader, but under his parka he had a big shiny police badge. I played it cool, having grown up watching that scene in *The Great Escape* every Boxing Day. The one where the guard wishes Gordon Jackson 'Good Luck' in English as he gets on the bus. A few minutes later the bad cop turned up, dressed in a leather greatcoat and bulging briefcase. He spent an unnatural amount of time comparing me to my photograph and he clearly prided himself in looking very severe. He didn't even smile at my Christmas decorations. Bah, humbug!

This morning, rather embarrassingly, I sleep in. So as the train pulls into Ulan Bator at 06:30 I'm still snoring in my bunk, oblivious to the excitement of a new country. I had wanted to have a look around UB, even if I didn't get far outside the station. Instead I sleep. In fact I sleep through several stops in the morning, not rising until our brief stop at a place called Choyr around midday. This surprises me, as I have been getting up at first light each morning. I really feel that my body needs some extra time to recharge after days of time zone changes and nocturnal sweats.

Our stop in Choyr is actually one of the high

points of the trip so far. I can only explain my elation at being there as being about living in the moment in a seriously remote part of the world. After my first proper sleep for a few days, here I am with some great fellow travellers in the middle of the Gobi desert. Despite the low temperatures, the bright sun and intense clear sky somehow warm my soul, if not my limbs. In that single moment I feel that life can't get much better.

Choyr is actually a fair-sized city, but the station makes it feel small and insignificant. The only serious historical fact I learned was that it is home to the first Mongolian cosmonaut: there is a statue of him right behind the station. Major-General Jügderdemidiin Gürragchaa is a Hero of the Soviet Union. His capsule returned to earth on 22 March 1981, after seven days in space.

So after getting some sunshine and a few lungfuls of chilly air, I take lunch with Stephan and Ceyda. I don't think she knows yet about his plans for free love amongst an enlarged group of like-minded adults, but I'm not going to say anything. Instead I reflect on how I have been turning a bit more native each day that I have spent on the train. For example, I don't care that my new Mongolian next door neighbours have left their vegetable scrapings in my bathroom sink this morning. I drink (cooled) water from the train samovar, and now actually quite like how it tastes. I'm also communicating in international sign language at an advanced level, and don't mind making a fool of myself. This isn't a lifestyle where you should feel embarrassed about such things. I also can't stop myself ordering anything now without pointing at it and holding up the number of fingers to indicate how many of it I want, and miming the temperature I expect it to arrive at.

Back to what's been going on today. There have been some big changes overnight while I have been sleeping. The train has filled up a lot at UB. Half a dozen Mongolian carriages have been added to the train and pair of brightly coloured locomotives up front are now hauling us. The railway in Mongolia is diesel, and after electric power across Russia, the engines sound very different. The carriage that was all my own I now share with about six other passengers – all, I assume, to be 'posh' first class Mongolians. The traders are all further forward in the Mongolian equivalent of second class.

The most significant change of all is the arrival of the Mongolian restaurant car. Just to try and catch me out they have placed it in the middle of the train, but only about two carriages (or ten doors) away. I must now turn right, rather than left, from my compartment. The new restaurant is very different from the Russian one. It must be one of the top ten train restaurant cars in the world, even if only for its originality. It's covered in wooden carvings and has a range of musical instruments and hunting memorabilia hanging on the walls. It's heated to about 35°C, and the lady who runs it speaks some English. Best of all, she smiles and looks pleased to see her customers. Deep joy.

Having only just woken up, whilst my travelling companions drink icy Altan Gobi beer with their soup, I sample my first cup of Mongolian coffee. This is strong enough to power the motor of a V2 rocket, and soon has me spinning into the new time zone. Brunch turns into a leisurely and very social couple of hours, the warmth inside, the European chat and the blue sky all seeming a bit of an escape from the bleakness of Siberia. Outside now is just a vast open landscape of desert.

I pay for my lunch in rubles. It turns out that you can pay in almost any currency you want. This was good, as I had no tugriks, and would not now need to enlist the services of the black market traders to get some.

Getting back to Carriage no 9 has some new challenges today. Between the restaurant and my home are a couple of newly installed carriages of Mongolian first class. The first thing that I notice passing through is a large sign on the carriage door prohibiting the letting off of fireworks inside the carriage. That's nice and clear, and good to know next time I'm thinking of packing some bangers on a future adventure in Mongolia.

The Mongolian carriages look quite plush and are heated to a temperature you would find in a provincial hotel sauna. They have a slightly weird smell, but then again so does my carriage – and probably so do I after a week living on this train. Other than the fireworks, there is another important lesson to learn in Trans-Mongolian safety here. The carriages have a really tricky bridge arrangement as you cross between them. It's harder than the Russian or Chinese cars, and you must grab a low handle on the other side before stepping across.

On the way back to Carriage no 9, I bump into Mr Chen, who is talking to some of the Chinese guards in Carriage no 11. He is all smiles today, and amazingly hands me his official door keys so that he doesn't need to follow me back to let me in. It is quite an honour to be trusted with 'the' real Chinese Railway key, clearly a sign of diplomatic progress after the incident a few days ago. I would be ashamed if he knew that I didn't actually need his key to get back in. Chen has been generally very friendly to me, and I find his approach just right to the novice Trans-Mongolian traveller. Li on the other hand is a man who does his job well, but would prefer that there were no passengers involved in the process.

The day spins by. I'm listening to my back catalogue of Pink Floyd albums whilst writing and taking photographs from my compartment. Outside new and exotic things pass by like camels and clusters of colourful traditional tents, known here as 'gers'. This is totally different from southern Siberia, just twelve hours away.

Late in the afternoon we stop at an armpit of a place called Sain-Shanda. It consists of a single long and filthy platform, where traders sell food from makeshift stalls. Rubbish is piled up all over the place, and mangy dogs scrabble amongst the mess. We're about 20 minutes late getting here, but there is no coal for us to load. This explains why we added extra supplies in Siberia yesterday. The air is now seriously dry, and there is no longer any sign of snow, despite the low temperature. The locals here look quite different from the Russians; their features are Asian and their skin is a healthy-looking dark brown colour. They have embedded smiles on their faces and seem pretty friendly towards people like me.

Without the coal loading to indicate our re-supply progress, I am caught out by a sudden and totally unannounced departure. Out of sight of Mr Chen, I'm doing my trainspotter bit at the engine end when the doors suddenly slam shut up and down the train. I have to get back on the train, and right away. Having thought about this the other day, I perform my emergency getting-back-on drill – in this case onto a Mongolian second class carriage about 100 metres away from my own. I'm not going to risk being left in Sain-

Shanda at any cost, so I dive up some thankfully unmanned steps and return to my carriage inside the train. I had wondered if Li or Chen would have notice I was not on board and hold the train, but they didn't – proof that ultimately I'm on my own and have to be self-reliant at all times. By now I always carry my day bag containing my documents wherever I go. I once read a story of an American lady who missed her train and was left behind, but due to having good party connections was given a lift in a fast car and managed to catch it up again. It's a good story, but looking round here at the cars, that really would be an adventure.

Back in my compartment, staring out once again at the frozen Gobi, I am reminded of the moment when Mrs Richards complains of the view from her *Fawlty Towers* bedroom window. Basil would be in his element here – I can see herds of yak and horses sweeping majestically across the plain as the sun dips behind the distant hills. Even though there are no hanging gardens of Babylon, it's a great view nonetheless.

In the restaurant car there is an impromptu meeting of the Train 004 European Travellers' Club. We will reach the Chinese border this evening, and it's a final chance to try some more of the dishes on the Mongolian menu. The rather excellent dumplings have sold out by the time I arrive, but I manage to get the 'Traveller's Beef', which is pretty good. Rubles will be useless tomorrow, so I enquire about the range of alcoholic beverages in stock. The restaurant manager shows me to her secret stash, and I'm amazed to discover a selection of dusty wine bottles and even some cheap Russian 'champanski'. I'm just about to buy a bottle of rather overpriced French wine when I find a bottle of interesting-looking Armenian red at the back of the cupboard. With that saving made, I buy the champanski too.

Just like yesterday, there is an atmosphere amongst travellers of mingled apprehension about another night of border games ahead, and sadness that we are leaving Mongolia so soon. This is a great restaurant car, and full credit to Mongolian Railways for making it a unique way to market their country to their passengers. The drill tonight will be to detach all the Mongolian carriages together with the restaurant before we reach the Chinese frontier. Playing it safe after my earlier brush with disaster, I return to the Chinese part of the train well before we reach the border post at Dzamynude.

I make it back through Mongolian first class without any firework-related incidents and cross over the final jump between carriages with my wine. My first job is to stash the champanski in my minibar, and put it out in the end of the carriage. I hide it under a sack of coal that has been provided by the Japanese Red Cross. I'm not quite sure how that has come about, but give it a couple of hours and it should be nicely chilled.

Back at my HQ, there is a new bundle of paperwork to complete. Amongst the red tape are two tickets to a complimentary breakfast in the Chinese restaurant car at 06:00 tomorrow morning. I guess that my breakfast is free, as the Chinese state railway runs it as well as operating my carriage. As I have two berths in my compartment, I technically have two train tickets and I am therefore also entitled to two breakfasts. I have my suspicions about the composition of a Chinese railway breakfast, but put them on hold for now. Time to get my pen out and start form-filling.

Now familiar with the drill, I find myself sat in my compartment in the silence and semi-darkness at Dzamynude, waiting for the customs and immigration process to begin. It doesn't seem quite as intense as yesterday's border crossing, but once again I'm visited by dozens of officials. Mr Li and Mr Chen are on their best behaviour; I assume this is because they are returning to their home country and have to look a bit more respectable. I'm stamped out of Mongolia (I only had a transit visa that lasted 48 hours – just as well I didn't get left behind at Sain-Shanda) and we trundle towards China to repeat the stamping.

I realise at this point that my fizzy Russian wine might be getting too cold and I don't want it to freeze. On the other hand, I don't think I'm supposed to leave my compartment, and I don't want to bump into a Chinese customs officer when I'm armed with a box of illicit booze. Checking furtively in the corridor for signs of movement, I decide to go for it. I make it to the outer door successfully, but sure enough I meet a Chinese official in the corridor coming back. Bugger. He stares at me and I grin back, nodding my head in the closest thing to a bow that I judge might be appropriate in the circumstances. Nothing is said and he doesn't look too surprised, so I just duck back into my compartment. Those in the carriage will have heard a popping noise about 5 minutes later. The champanski is sweet, but very cold. I have a little solo celebration to mark my first successful crossing of the Gobi.

The Mongolian police seem fairly relaxed, and the Chinese officials have no issues with my paperwork. I think they have seen it all before, and are much more interested in the traders and black market smugglers in the other carriages. With the red tape finished and another visa stamped in my passport, there is an option to get off the train and wait in the station. I'm suspicious about this, as we need to swap wheels here to match the narrower four foot eight and a half inch gauge of the Chinese tracks, and this could take several hours. Most of the Mongolians leave the train and those that remain lumber off to a big shed close by. The process is similar to entering Belarus, but the driver of the shunter seems to care much less for his passengers – the carriages are peeled off one by one and each time a carriage is uncoupled he smashes into it with such force that anything not fixed to the floor gets thrown about. I brace myself across the seat and hang on to my minibar.

Day Fourteen, Erlian, China
Distance travelled so far: 10,261 km

Beijing time (GMT+8)

Station	Arrival	Stop	Departure
Erlian	21:00	237	00:57
Zhunhe	03:08	2	03:10
Jning	05:47	9	05:56
Datong	07:59	12	08:11
Zhangjiakou	10:36	10	10:46
Beijing	14:04		

At about 01:00 the train is reassembled and we are pushed back onto the platform at Erlian. Clearly the Chinese want to make a good impression, as there is a coloured light show, with patriotic music played over the public address system, and soldiers stand to attention, their rifles ported for inspection. As the music finishes they salute the train, and we pull out into the darkness of rural China. Time for bed.

I don't make it to either of my two breakfasts after discovering that they will only be served between 06:00 and 07:00. I hear from those who went that it consisted of a hard-boiled egg, plain rice and tea. Instead I sleep in and once up, potter about, sorting out my gear. In the absence of any sign of Li or Chen, I head off to where I guess the restaurant car might be for lunch at the crazy Chinese time of 11:00. I have no problem finding the carriage, but I'm greeted by a very different world to the one where I have enjoyed Russian or Mongolian meals. The first thing I notice is how cold it is, followed closely by the weird smell of unfamiliar culinary delights. The carriage is also laid out differently from the others. At the kitchen end there is a lady managing the ticket system. She allocates seats at tables based on her view of your suitability to dine with others. Next to her is a hatch through to the kitchen and an impressive display of Chinese alcohol, dominated by bottles of Great Wall wine. At the table behind her sits a lady with large calculator and a pile of money. Finally, if this isn't all a bit much, behind her stands a man wearing a police uniform. I'm not sure if there's the risk of any possible noodle theft going on, but I obviously feel safer knowing that he's there to look after my lunch.

The restaurant is busy with Chinese people eating industrial quantities of noodles and strange balls made of something that I can't quite identify. They don't seem to take much notice of my arrival. This is good – nothing's worse than one of those moments when everyone stops eating and stares at you. I learn later that the pricing of a Chinese restaurant car is designed to be very affordable, so it's busy with locals. The carriage is also packed, as the car only opens for short periods to serve meals – gone is the open-all-hours approach and social centre I have had up until now. Outside of opening hours the carriage becomes a private staff room dedicated to smoking and drinking tea.

I hand my special ticket over and I'm directed to a nearby table where the other *farangs* are. By good fortune Stephan and Ceyda are already sat here. They are both dressed in coats and wearing woollen hats. Yesterday such behaviour would have been quite mad, but the climate is now pretty chilly. They have discovered this at breakfast and returned for lunch properly dressed. The news is mixed. Stephan is travelling in first class and Ceyda in *kupe* (in Chinese, second class soft). Their romance has been going well, but last night the RSM has banned further visits by Ceyda to Stephan's compartment, as her ticket does not allow her to be in a first class carriage. I point out that I have two tickets and Ceyda could use my spare one, but I think the magic moment has been missed.

There is no menu or choice of what we are going to be served. Within a few seconds of our sitting down, chicken balls are delivered to us (not testicles, but chicken meat in dollops, so to speak) on plastic plates, with rice and vegetables. I think this is very much the 'dish of the day' for those on the ticket system. I add soy sauce with abandon to try and perk up the incredible blandness of the food, but it doesn't work. A week on this diet would be a disaster, and I'm glad I will soon be in Beijing.

As this is the final meal, there is talk of where people are headed next. I don't know many of them very well, but there is a definite bond of shared experience. The Finnish girls, Christina and Anna, are bound for a beach in Thailand, the Germans are headed on to the Burmese border by train (reported closed), and Ceyda is heading back to the United States. Stephan is flying ahead of me on to Shanghai. There is a sort of end-of-tour party feel to our lunch. In just a few hours we will scatter, mainly bound for hot showers in a variety of hotels and guesthouses across Beijing.

Back in Carriage no 9 I spend the last few hours packing my stuff up whilst looking out at yet another new landscape. We are now in the middle of a mountain range and the rail tracks have been carved through the rock as we cross the huge gorges and pass hydro-electric power plants. In the distance there are tall red and white painted chimneys partially hidden behind a layer of smog. Leaving Inner Mongolia behind, the route takes us through endless mountain tunnels towards Hebei Province.

Our penultimate stop is in Datong, a modern industrialised Chinese city. This was once the stopping-off point for camel caravans on the way to Mongolia. Today it's the stopping-off point for those planning on building more cement factories or petrochemical plants. The outskirts reveal the vast differences in living standards and ways of life of old and new China. I find that arriving in any city by train tends to reveal this – by its very nature, living next to a railway line isn't a popular choice, but rather an economic necessity. It often showcases the underclasses and the worst architecture that a city has to offer. My first and only impression of Datong is that I can see no reason to linger. It looks just like the way many northern Chinese cities look to me. Miles of rust and concrete inhabited by armies of busy people on the move.

On Platform 3 it is immediately clear that much polishing of uniform has taken place overnight. The train crew are now dressed up like they are on a passing out parade at Sandhurst, overseen of course by the sergeant major. All the guards are out on the platform standing to attention by the carriage doors. This seems bizarre, as no one is actually getting on or off the train – the enormous platform is deserted. Are we performing some sort of dress rehearsal for our arrival in Beijing? I breathe in the smog for a couple of minutes, enjoying the new sensation of alienation of being a *farang* in a Chinese railway station. I decide to head to the front of the train for a photograph, but the local station guards must think I'm a madman and shout at me to get back to my carriage. This is enough of Datong for me, so I get back on board the train.

Mr Chen and Mr Li have spent the morning preparing the carriage and cleaning various bits of the train, many of those for the first time since we left Moscow. They look happy, and with good reason – Mr Li says that they have three days' leave before heading back to Moscow on Train 003, the same train travelling in the opposite direction. They are an odd couple, but I can see how they work well together as a team. Their job isn't an easy one and at times it can be a brutal way of life, with the coal, the frozen doors and the ice on the underneath of the carriage to sort out several times each day. Somehow opposites work well here, but I would be surprised if they go out for a drink together in Beijing.

Rather miraculously my belongings fit back in my bags. Living in such a small space I have become something of an expert in storing things in every nook and cranny of the compartment. The trick now is to remember where everything is hidden. I have quite a lot of stuff that is surplus to requirements, and Ceyda helps me donate all my unused food and sundries to a lovely but hard-up

Mongolian family that she is sharing a compartment with. I don't think they will like my Russian instant noodles, but put them in the goody bag as well, just in case.

With my bags packed, I sit back and try not to get too depressed about leaving this amazing train in just a few hours' time. I had forgotten how many bags I have. At least they are lighter now, without the Siberian rations and my minibar.

I have a glimpse of the future as we pass through the suburbs of Beijing. Our old-fashioned Trans-Mongolian train looks totally out of context as we pass through Beijing South railway station. Ours is the only scruffy diesel-powered train with dull green carriages in a world of gleaming white ultra-high-speed electric trains. In a few days' time I will be sampling this world for myself. Perhaps in deference to how out of place we look in this futuristic station, our driver doesn't stop in Beijing South, but continues to the older main station. I feel for him. This is the railway equivalent of a Douglas C-47 passing by a fleet of Airbus A380s. A wormhole in train time.

The centre of Beijing must be more than an hour from its outskirts. We finally pull into Beijing's main, rather old-fashioned, central station in downtown Dongcheng at just after 14:00 local time. It is the Beijing equivalent of Euston, on Chinese steroids. Porters rush up and down the platforms with piles of luggage on trolleys.

Vendors manoeuvre impressively large carts of noodles to arriving trains, weaving in and out of the army of people on the move.

It's the end of the line for this train. Not wishing to hurry, I let the other passengers get off first. Li and Chen don't feel the same; they're only too happy to escape, and as soon as they have unloaded the bedding they meet up with the other guards on the platform to smoke and compare notes. Before they escape I give them each a small bottle of Scotch and wish them well.

I spot Stephan and Ceyda on the platform and we agree to take a farewell photograph at the front of the train. I'm glad about this as I wanted to take one of the locomotive anyway, and now I have an excuse to walk the twenty carriages or so without looking like a sad and solitary train-spotter. We have completed the final leg of the Trans-Mongolian route with a Chinese engine. It has sort of a 1980s diesel intercity look about it. With the photographs done we split up, having agreed to meet for Christmas dinner tomorrow. I have four days' R&R now, before catching a very different sort of train to Shanghai.

Ten: Nine Million Bicycles

Day Fourteen, Beijing, China
Distance travelled so far: 11,112 km

I'm quite surprised how I have become so used to living inside the confines of the Trans-Mongolian train; living in a box smaller than a prison cell and without running water. I had even almost acclimatised to the extremes of temperature, both hot and cold. But now I'm the proverbial bird that has flown its cage. I am alone, about to launch myself into millions of people on bicycles in a strange city. My initial feeling is that it is going to be an exciting place, and it smells of noodles in a good way. Not being able to recognise most of the signs, I follow the tide of people into a tunnel under the tracks and out to the station exit. I have arranged for someone to meet me and hold my hand, but there is no sign of them. With hindsight it's a bad idea anyway – how would you spot someone in a station so huge?

My luggage doesn't seem to draw much attention here. In fact, having lots of luggage looks to be a prerequisite for a long-range Chinese rail passenger. I make my way through the security barrier and emerge into the world outside. Here there are hawkers, touts and travellers all mixed together in a seething mass of people. Police are everywhere, checking identity papers. Then I see a man in a dark suit, dark tie and crisp white shirt. He has already spotted me, and strides over to help, brushing off the touts and taking most of my baggage. He shows me across the square to his double-parked black Mercedes with blacked-out windows. With the bags stowed, he passes me a cold towel and a freshly pressed copy of today's *China Daily* newspaper. Sitting in the leather upholstered back seat, I consider for the first time just how grubby and dishevelled I must look. I now resemble a hobo in a limousine, perhaps a bit like Dan Aykroyd in *Trading Places*. I feel so embarrassed about this that I feel that I am going to have to explain the reason for my appearance when I get to my hotel.

I don't know how many tramps check into business hotels, but the immaculately dressed staff at the reception desk pretend not to notice how I look and possibly smell. I can only assume that as long as my credit card is working, all is well. A concierge whisks me up to my floor in the futuristic lift. He speaks some English, and I try to explain why I look the way I do. I'm not convinced that he understands, but he presses on with a demonstration of some of the gadgets in my room and then leaves me to admire my view out over to the CCTV building – the second biggest office space in the world after the Pentagon.

Alone in my room I survey my new surroundings. The bed alone is bigger than my compartment on the Trans-Mong. My toes actually sink into the deep pile of the carpet and the room is totally still – no rocking or swaying whatsoever. I'm so excited I don't know what to do first, but decide to turn on the big plasma television and search for a news channel in English to see what has been going on in the world. Then I strip off – carefully placing my clothes in a laundry bag, in case they might contaminate the room.

The bathroom is a temple of cleanliness, a cathedral of ablution. It has a walk-in shower and a computer-controlled toilet that at first scares me after becoming so used to the simplicity of Trans-Siberian plumbing. I jab at a few buttons, guessing their purpose. Lights flash and water squirts at me. The seat has a mind of its own, lowering when it senses my presence and heating itself up. I need to study the manual if I can find one in English. My first job is to remove a couple of weeks of beard with a pair of scissors. I have seen Harrison Ford do this in *The Fugitive*, but I have to tell you it takes much longer to remove a beard in real life. I liked the film, but I'm not a fan of Tommy Lee Jones.

After much scrubbing, I emerge about two hours later feeling like (and hopefully looking like) a different person. I dress in the best clothes I have (still not smart enough for this place), and head downstairs for a drink. Outside the bar stands a huge Christmas tree, and a Chinese Santa dressed in a weird green outfit. At a seat at the bar I quaff expensive beers and tell tales of long-range rail adventure to world-wise expats with big cigars. Things catch up with me all too quickly, though, and I realise that I urgently need some proper sleep.

Twelve hours later I wake to discover that we are not moving. My brain takes a moment to decode the reason why, and I confirm my suspicions by extending my arms and legs as far as I can. My bed is so big that I can't find its edges in any direction. This is not a train. It's a hotel. Padding over to my desk, I find that there is a button to open the curtains. On the desk is a courier delivery that I hadn't spotted yesterday. It contains some tickets in Chinese and a hand-written letter from a local travel agent who has sorted out my next journey. In all the excitement of running water and five star bedding, I'd forgotten all about having saved myself unnecessary worry – the tickets are here. I put the envelope in with my other travel documents. I have been using a folder of plastic wallets in chronological order, so it's easy to locate anything at speed at a station or on a border. This done, I text the agent and thank her for sorting out exactly what I had requested. Another piece of the jigsaw is complete.

This is possibly my weirdest Christmas Day ever. I spend the morning wandering by myself around the Forbidden City. It's cold (in a non-Siberian way), and the buildings are lit up by an intense blue sunshine. China does not celebrate Christmas in the religious sense, but it has become a big thing: all the restaurants, shopping malls and hotels are packed with implausible Santa impersonators. In the Forbidden City, though, I am completely removed from the commercialism.

However stunning and unusual my surroundings, I'm missing Christmas at home – the pub, the roast potatoes and the classic movies on television. I can't decide if it is better to try and forget that it is Christmas, or to do Christmas as best as I can here in China. I opt for the latter. Sat on a bench near the Hall of Supreme Harmony, I text Christmas messages to my family and friends, forgetting that most will still be in bed.

The plan for the evening was to have Christmas dinner with Stephan and Ceyda at a place famous for its Peking duck, called Da Dong. Impressing myself with my grasp of the metro system, I arrive early and swap texts with Stephan. He is waiting at Da Dong too; it just happens to be a different one, and Ceyda is at a third one. It takes about an hour to get us all to one restaurant, and we eventually have a four-course meal of many delicacies, including a roast duck carved at our table by a man dressed in rubber gloves and a facemask. He's not taking any chances on what he might catch from us.

After dinner we find a place to drink tea and compare notes on our Beijing experiences. Ceyda is off tomorrow to stay with a family who live in a town near the Great Wall of China. I decide not to tell her about my hotel room. Stephan is breaking the rules of the long-distance rail adventurer and flying to Shanghai in the morning. This leaves me alone in Beijing for a couple more days.

The bill in the teashop is 500 yuan (£60) for three cups of warm water with some dead leaves in. It turns out that I have fallen for the classic Chinese tourist tea ceremony scam. Stephan suggests that worse things could have happened on our trip, which is a fair point. I'm still annoyed with myself for not spotting it sooner. I decide not to kick up a fuss, because of the gang of excitable triads with meat cleavers waiting behind the back door if we were to leg it. Outside, the taxis are ignoring me; so instead I get into a bizarre cart that resembles the *Hong Kong Phooey* mobile from the 1970s television cartoon. The advantage of this is the driver seems to be bound by no road laws and we cross over pavements and through one-way streets the wrong way to save time. The disadvantage is that there are no safety features whatsoever, and if anything were to hit us I doubt it would be survivable. Outside the hotel they can see that the English tramp is back, as I pull up in my Phooey mobile.

Day Sixteen, Beijing, China
Distance covered so far: 11,112 km

After a couple of days being a tourist it's time to think about the next leg of my journey. Like Martin Sheen in his Saigon hotel room in *Apocalypse Now* (one of my favourite films), I don't want to get too comfortable in my room. A long-distance rail traveller should be on a train. When I pack up my bags once more, I seem to have a lot less stuff than I did in Moscow: I have jettisoned heat shields, chopping boards, pee bottles and assorted other things I felt I would never need again. Not for this adventure anyway. I could write a book about packing for this adventure, and maybe one day I will.

What lie ahead are two trains, both a world

away from what I have experienced so far. My biggest concern with the next leg is not the train itself, but finding it. The Chinese way of doing things is different from the rest of Asia. The huge stations use a unique system of waiting rooms. Furthermore, the sheer numbers of passengers are huge – I can see myself getting lost, crushed or left behind if I'm not on the ball.

Perhaps keen to make sure I leave Beijing, my hotel sends a concierge with me to the station. Chris is a renaissance Chinaman, and can speak half a dozen languages whilst simultaneously programming instructions into his various mobile devices. Total overkill, but it makes my induction into Chinese railway station navigation very easy. I'm sorry to confess that I also use him as my Passepartout, letting him carry a bag about the same size and weight as he is. Sagging under the load as we leave the car, he politely suggests that a bag with wheels would be good, and I agree with him. The next time I travel on the Trans-Mongolian I will get a bag that has wheels.

The first hurdle of Chinese railway travel is being allowed into the station. I have to queue up behind an excitable bunch of Chinese holiday-makers. Rather than crowd me out, they seem to take pity on me as a lone *farang*, and actually make a space for me to slip in towards the front of the queue. A timely reminder to me that it is all too easy for the traveller to start judging people based on limited experiences and preconceptions.

At the front of the queue I present my documents and am allowed inside. Chris puts the bags onto the X-ray machine belt like a weightlifter that has just achieved his personal best but might never lift that weight again. The entrance hall is massive, and streams of people march like ants in all directions without running into each other. Welcome to Beijing South, the biggest railway station in China.

Chris has decided that I am either a VIP (or, more likely, special needs) and has found a suitable lounge to leave me in. I'm not sure if I'm entitled to be there, but he's clearly a fixer and I conclude that anyone arriving here with his own batman probably justifies entry. A team of elegant Chinese ladies dressed in long red coats run the lounge. Whilst I find a seat, he organises a station porter to come and collect the luggage and get me onto the train to Shanghai Hongqiao. We say goodbye to each other and I promise that if we ever meet again I will have wheels on my bags.

In the lounge I sit back and drink tea until a porter comes to fetch me – he knows where we're going, even if I don't. I follow him across the station concourse, weaving in and out of the crowds in the space behind him and his trolley. Nearby is Gate 13, where several hundred people are lining up to get past the barrier and onto the platform. The porter heads straight to the front of the queue, says something to the ticket inspector and pointing in my direction. He then gets my bags into a lift. All I have to do is pay a small fee to the man on the barrier and I have completely avoided the anarchy of boarding.

The doors of the lift open, and ahead of us on the platform is a sleek and new-looking CRH3 train painted in China Railway Corporation cream and blue. My train today is the G15, which will travel at over 300 kph to reach Shanghai, over 1,300 km away, in less than five hours. The Trans-Mongolian takes twenty-four hours to cover the same distance. (Or for an example closer to home, the G15 goes at twice the speed of the Edinburgh to London train, which takes about five hours to cover just 632 km.) Today, China has the largest high-speed rail network in the world, with over 1.4 billion people travelling on its 20,000 km of high-speed tracks each year. It's also growing rapidly: just a few days ago a service was launched from Beijing to Guangzhou, cutting the journey time from twenty-four hours to ten.

I'm greeted at the pointy end of Carriage 16 by a conductress who is clearly fresh out of Chinese Train finishing school. She shows me through a glass sliding door and into a private compartment. In the nose of the train are five big leather seats in a section called VIP class. It has the feel of a private jet about it, and there is so much room that I can put all my bags in front of my seat, even with the seat in full flat bed mode. I fear this will never catch on with rail operators back home.

The porter leaves me to play with the gadgets, and sitting in my seat I began to get quite excited about take-off. From my chair I can see where the driver sits, and he isn't on the train yet. There is an LED panel above our seats counting down to blast off – 5 minutes to go. The carriage remains empty, apart from one other person who sits opposite me. I assume he is a businessman off to sell something big and shiny to someone in Shanghai. At 10:57 the doors of the carriage slide closed, and with a gentle whir of motors we ease backwards out of the station. I now realise the reason for there being no driver is that I'm at the rear of the train. It has a pointy carriage at both ends. Our take-off is notable only for its smooth-ness, and we progressively increase speed. About 10 minutes into the journey we pass 300 kph, but there is hardly any movement inside. The train is totally smooth and very quiet. Looking back up the tracks, it's like one of those train document-aries where the film has speeded up. Large build-ings quickly shrink and vanish from my view.

I decide to explore my new Buck Rogers world. Next to VIP class is a section containing business class. This is confusing as it is identical to VIP class except for it being wider, with three seats across. Further down in the next coach is first class, which looks a bit basic compared the leather and personal TV screens of business class. Passengers chat, sleep, make instant noodles and watch the world speeding by. The LED display shows the time, the temperature outside and our next stop. At our time-machine-like speed I see the temperature rise by several degrees each hour. China is defrosting as we speed southwards.

My lunch is simple but tasty. There is no choice; I am presented with a microwaved beef and duck medley with noodle soup in a plastic box. No tea or coffee, just water or Coke. It seems strange to me to spend so much on the hardware of futuristic trains but not to offer a decent meal. We stop briefly at Jinan West and then Nanjing South en route to Shanghai. The stations are all brand new shiny temples of rail. I let countryside flash past to a soundtrack of *The Very Best of Japan*, which seems to fit my surroundings rather well.

Late in the afternoon we arrive on time into a misty and murky Shanghai Hongqiao station. Like Beijing South, it is modern and massive inside. Avoiding the touts with some ease, I join the queue and get a proper taxi towards the Bund.

My driver has been in training for the next Chinese Grand Prix. His Changan 1.6 litre car lacks Formula One balance, though, and our braking and cornering leave much to be desired.

At first the streets of Shanghai look similar to Beijing to my untrained eye. It takes about half an hour to reach the Bund, where we pull up outside my hotel. My fingers have been clenched on the headrest of the passenger seat in front to deal with the G force of deceleration, and I leave a permanent imprint as I extract myself from the back of the car.

My hotel is old school, a throwback to Shanghai's colonial past. In the bar a group of old Chinese men play jazz music to an appreciative audience. After a couple of pleasant hours I retire to my bedroom and open the window to let some fresh air in – an unknown pleasure on the Trans-Mongolian train. A few minutes pass until I'm startled by a deafening 'boinnnnggg'. No one has thought to mention that the hotel has a bell tower whose bell rings every 15 minutes of the day and night. I count the boings through the night, and check out the following morning when I've counted seven boings. All sorts of upgrades are offered, but I take the moral position that it's too late to be bribed, and check into a modern high-rise hotel on the other side of the Bund.

Eleven: Empire of the Sun

Day Seventeen, Shanghai, China
Distance travelled so far: 12,430 km

Next door to my new hotel is the world's tallest (roof occupied) building – the Bottle Opener, or to give it its correct title, the Shanghai World Financial Centre. I decide to take in the view and pay 150 RMB for a trip to its 100th floor sky bridge. This isn't my best decision, and I spend the next 20 minutes hanging onto the railings for dear life. The floor is made of glass, and school-kids jump up and down on it trying to see if they can break through without considering the con-sequences. I am relieved to make it back down again. It's much nicer being on the ground wish-ing you're up in the air than up in the air wishing you're down on the ground.

Slightly freaked out by my high-altitude experience, I decide not to dine that night in the revolving restaurant near the top of the nearby Oriental Pearl Tower. It's an amazing futurist design from the 1990s, but I'm happier to look across at it from nearer the ground, seeing it as it appears on the front cover of this book. Instead I take a drink on the comparatively much lower 26th floor of my hotel. With no glass underfoot, I feel almost normal again. But my mind must be playing tricks as I think I can feel movement. The bar manager tells me not to worry – the hotel is designed to sway in high winds and earthquakes. He points out that there are no lights hanging from the ceiling, so that most people won't notice the occasional sway. My senses must have become super-heightened lately.

My brief stay in Shanghai passes too quickly, and tomorrow my epic adventure comes to an end. My regret at this point is that I'm headed further south to Hong Kong, but on an aircraft. I wish now that I had arranged to get there by rail, but I didn't know when I set off how I would be feeling by this stage. Hong Kong would be a good destination to aim for in a future trip, and I make a note of this in my journal. I now need to reconfigure my luggage for flying. Back in my room I repack my bags yet again, this time discarding anything I can to fit within the 20 kg luggage allowance. The only way I am going to achieve this is to wear as much as I can and throw away anything of low value. Once I've packed I lie in bed and contemplate my final train journey the next morning. I have saved the fastest and most exotic train until last.

Day Eighteen, Shanghai, China
Distance travelled so far: 12,490 km.

Today is all about speed. I am going to take the Maglev, currently the fastest train in the world, if in fact you can call it a train. The Shanghai Maglev has been operating (at a huge loss) since 2004. It runs less than 20 per cent full, perhaps because the line does not actually reach the centre of the city – you have to take a bus or a taxi out to Longyang Road first, then get on the train.

I arrive at the station quite early for my final train journey. Timing is important today if I am going to achieve my goal and become the fastest rail passenger on Planet Earth. Between 09:00 and 10:45 each day the train runs a bit faster. For the rest of the day the power is turned down to save electricity. If I get on the right train I will hit a top speed of 430 kph, 130 kph faster than later on in the day. Like an early Apollo moon shot, my journey is going to be short one but quite exciting. The trip, just 30 kilometres long, will get me to the airport in less than 7 minutes.

I purchase a VIP ticket for RMB 80 (£8) and take the escalator up to the platform where I can see out over the raised line ahead, built on stilts every 25 metres or so. It isn't long before a train arrives back from the airport, and I have no problem getting on. I'm the only person in VIP class. Why would anyone other than me spend double the fare for the same experience with just a different-coloured seat and a touch of leather on a seven-minute journey? I settle in and wonder if special preparations might be needed for such ultra-high speed. I can't even see any seatbelts.

The VIP carriage is immediately behind the cockpit. There is a glass panel in front of me behind where the driver sits, so I too can see out over the track ahead. You might imagine that the driver of the fastest train in the world would be an elite pilot, perhaps dressed like the captain of an aircraft or even Buzz Lightyear. But sat in the driver's seat is a young man dressed in a hoodie, jeans and trainers. I must say, it's a bit of a *Wizard of Oz* moment. Unaware of my gaze, he's busy doing something on a personal device, perhaps working hard to improve his score on *Mortal Kombat*. I wonder if he should in fact be rather busier when preparing to take responsibility for my life on an ultra-high-speed rail line. His cabin is unremarkable, and there seem to be a few extras on the floor – is that a fan heater plugged in next to his feet? In 2006 one of these trains caught fire, so I wonder if a fan heater is an approved accessory.

After five minutes or so he finishes his game, adjusts his seat (more like an office desk chair) and presses some buttons – I hope he's the real driver, not an impostor. But he knows which buttons to press: the doors close, the train levitates, and we shoot off towards the airport at warp speed. Above my seat there is a speed readout in a futuristic lime green. In less than 2 minutes, we accelerate past my previous speed record of 303 kph. The sensation is amazing. It becomes hard to focus on any individual objects close to the train. The track banks round corners, and I can feel real G force. We are still accelerating. I watch the readout cross 400 kph and within a couple of minutes we have topped out at 430 kph – for a brief moment I have become the fastest first class train passenger in the world. (I can definitely lay claim to this, as I was the only passenger in VIP class that day, but you are unlikely to find it in the *Guinness Book of World Records*.) After a minute or so we edge back to a more suburban 300 kph, and then decelerate as we make our approach to Pudong International Airport. Mission accomplished. This is the finish line of my adventure.

* * *

I covered 12,490 km in a little less than three

weeks. On one level, like any significant travel experience, much of it felt better in the anticipation and the reflection than in the execution. But on another level, I'm already missing the zen of travel by rail. It would be hypocritical of me to be negative about travel by plane, but overland adventure has given me a wonderfully different perspective on the size of the world and the diversity of its people.

Over the next few minutes I had to get used to being an ex-long-range rail adventurer, as I was now at an airport. Pudong was a Chinese version of Heathrow, sprawling and not very friendly to anyone carrying baggage. I eventually made it to the check-in, dripping with sweat from carrying my bag over the assault course in my full Trans-Siberian uniform. The woman who checked me in for my flight to Hong Kong didn't bat an eye, but I bet that over her lunch she would be telling her friends about the weird foreigner she had checked in.

A couple of hours later, sat in the tiny window seat of the China Southern A320, I contemplated how things were going to be now, without the train. I made an immediate commitment to myself to use this experience as grounding for something bigger.

I hope that you have enjoyed reading about my first ever experiences of Trans-Mongolian life. If you have time, could you let me know what you thought of my book by writing a few words of feedback on Amazon? I would be very grateful. If you have any questions or want to read more about my other adventures, please do have a look at my website -

www.matthew-woodward.com

The Story Continues ...

Back at home, I wasn't convinced at first that I was ready to get back on the rails again, but then after just a few months at HQ I started to look back on my first trip across Siberia through increasingly rose-tinted spectacles. I was really missing the crazy people, the strange places and the mad weather. I wanted more. Colder? Yes! Harder? Yes! Longer? Yes please!

Tales of my adventures seemed to really interest those I shared them with. They were more meaningful to others than I had realised that they might be. This was, after all, something that any determined traveller could achieve if they wanted to. Ice axes, crampons, skis or sherpa levels of fitness are not needed. With a growing confidence, I felt that maybe this was more than a one-off journey – perhaps the start of something bigger. What would it take to become full-time rail adventurer? I spent a lot of my time reading travel books and thinking through where the next challenge might lie.

There were several options, but at that time only one of these was not on the 'don't even think about it' list of the Foreign & Commonwealth Office travel warnings. It was the route overland from the UK to Singapore. I thought a lot about it and wondered how hard it might prove to be. Then down at a local pub one evening I told a few friends that I was going to travel as far as it was possible to travel by train. This year. Now, I couldn't go back; my drinking reputation depended upon it.

Over the summer I worked out a route, once again across Siberia, and then south through China and South East Asia to Singapore – nearly 19,000 km away. It wasn't just the distance, but the route was more complex. I would travel through some more risky places too, the legendary Thai/ Cambodian border town of Poipet, the Chinese frontier with Vietnam at Dong Dang and Yala province in Southern Thailand. Oh and the small issue that Cambodia had no working railway. Inspiration came to me from one of my greatest heroes, Sir Nicholas Winton: 'If something isn't blatantly impossible, then there must be a way of doing it'.

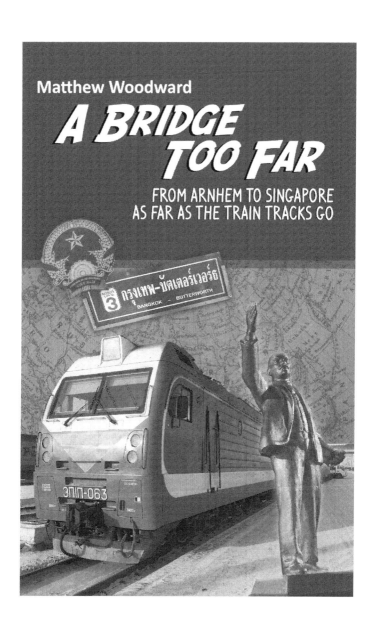

Matthew Woodward

A BRIDGE TOO FAR

FROM ARNHEM TO SINGAPORE
AS FAR AS THE TRAIN TRACKS GO

Filmography

(in order of appearance)

Midnight Express. Dir. Alan Parker. Columbia Pictures, 1978. Film.

Von Ryan's Express. Dir. Mark Robson. 20th Century Fox, 1965. Film.

Blackadder Goes Forth. Dir. John Lloyd. BBC, 1989. TV.

For Your Eyes Only. Dir. John Glen. United Artists, 1981. Film.

Fawlty Towers. Dir. John Howard Davies and Bob Spiers. BBC, 1975. TV.

Get Carter. Dir. Mike Hodges. Metro-Goldwyn-Mayer, 1971. Film.

The Great Escape. Dir. John Sturges. United Artists, 1963. Film.

The Hunt for Red October. Dir. John McTiernan. Paramount Pictures, 1990. Film.

Gorky Park. Dir. Michael Apted. Orion Pictures, 1983. Film.

Firefox. Dir. Clint Eastwood. Warner Brothers, 1982. Film.

The French Connection. Dir. William Friedkin. 20th Century Fox, 1971. Film.

Apollo 13. Dir. Ron Howard. Universal Pictures, 1995. Film.

Spies Like Us. Dir. John Landis. Warner Brothers, 1985. Film.

Trading Places. Dir. John Landis. Paramount Pictures, 1983. Film.

Apocalypse Now. Dir. Francis Coppola. United Artists, 1979. Film.

The Fugitive. Dir. *Andrew* Davis. Warner Brothers, 1993. Film.

Hong Kong Phooey. Dir. Charles A. Nichols. Taft Broadcasting, 1974. TV.

The Wizard of Oz. Dir. Victor Fleming. Loew's Inc, 1939. Film.

Acknowledgements

I'm grateful to all those who helped make my first Trans-Siberian adventure happen, and even more so to those who had the harder job of encouraging me to write a book about it.

To my great friend Keith Parsons, the man who told me I would be writing a book before I knew it myself. To Mark Smith, The Man in Seat Sixty-One, for giving me the knowledge and confidence to get back on the rails. To Dave Cornthwaite for encouraging me to say *yes* to the challenge. To Robert Twigger for helping me believe that I really should think of myself as an adventurer; and to Sir Ran Fiennes, for showing me the value of self-belief – he may not remember his words to me, but I shall never forget them.

To Alexey Samoylov, who taught me to think like a Russian. To Stefan and Ceyda, for being my Trans-Mongolian support network. To my long-range train travel-savvy friends and supporters: Roger Worrod, Rob Woodcock, Ian Pash, Sandy and Chris Willmott for keeping my spirits up on the move. To my team at Real Russia – Igor, Yuriy, Doina, Tanya, Stacy and Natasha – for sorting out the red tape and answering a thousand questions without complaint.

To Colonel Anand Swaroop for helping me get

started as a full-time adventurer. To Simon Rutter and Phil Anderton for their shared wisdom on the book world. To my colleague Mark Hudson for supporting my adventures around occasional bouts of agency work.

To Franz and the team at my base in Chiang Mai for keeping me in such a great frame of mind during the process of writing the book. To my editor, Caroline Petherick for her endless patience in sorting out my bad habits, and to Olga Tyukova, for turning some pretty mad ideas into lovely design and illustration.

Finally, to all the amazing people that I met who helped me on my journey. It doesn't matter if you don't speak a word of the same language; nearly all people in this world are innately kind and generous to strangers. Don't be put off travel by what you read in the newspapers.

About the Author

Matthew Woodward is a rail-based adventurer and writer. He has completed several Trans-Siberian, Trans-Mongolian and Trans-Manchurian rail journeys from his home in Edinburgh, reaching destinations such as Shanghai, Singapore, Tokyo and Hong Kong by train. In 2016 he successfully completed a solo journey on the longest and highest railways in the world, to reach Tibet by train.

He writes for a variety of media and publications on long-range train travel, and is a Fellow of the Royal Geographical Society. He is a self-confessed coffee addict and carries an espresso machine wherever he travels. *Trans-Siberian Adventures* is his first book.

For more information please visit
www.matthew-woodward.com

Printed in Great Britain
by Amazon